CITYSPOTS
BARCELONA

Teresa Fisher

Thomas Cook

KU-083-128

Written by Teresa Fisher
Original photography by Teresa Fisher
Front cover photography courtesy of Rosine Mazin/www.photolibrary.com
Series design based on an original concept by Studio 183 Limited

Produced by Cambridge Publishing Management Limited
Project Editor: Rachel Wood
Layout: Trevor Double
Maps: PC Graphics
Transport map: © Communicarta Ltd

Published by Thomas Cook Publishing
A division of Thomas Cook Tour Operations Limited
Company Registration No. 1450464 England
PO Box 227, Unit 18, Coningsby Road
Peterborough PE3 8SB, United Kingdom
email: books@thomascook.com
www.thomascookpublishing.com
+ 44 (0) 1733 416477
ISBN-13: 978-1-84157-612-1
ISBN-10: 1-84157-612-3

First edition © 2006 Thomas Cook Publishing
Text © 2006 Thomas Cook Publishing
Maps © 2006 Thomas Cook Publishing
Series Editor: Kelly Anne Pipes
Project Editor: Ross Hilton
Production/DTP: Steven Collins

Printed and bound in Spain by GraphyCems

CONTENTS

SYMBOLS & ABBREVIATIONS

The following symbols are used throughout this book:

ⓐ address ⓣ telephone ⓕ fax ⓔ email ⓦ website address
ⓞ opening times ⓝ public transport connections ⓘ important

The following symbols are used on the maps:

ⓘ information office　　　　○ city
✈ airport　　　　　　　　○ large town
✚ hospital　　　　　　　　○ small town
Ⓒ police station　　　　　═ motorway
▣ bus station　　　　　　─ main road
▤ railway station　　　　　minor road
Ⓜ metro　　　　　　　　─ railway
✝ cathedral
❶ numbers denote featured cafés & restaurants

Hotels and restaurants are graded by approximate price as follows:
£ budget　££ mid-range　£££ expensive

▶ *La Sagrada Familia – a work in progress*

Introduction

No other city is quite like Barcelona – this vibrant capital of Catalonia is dynamic, stylish and innovative, and boasts some of the finest and most eccentric art and architecture in the world. Its unique urban landscape resembles a living museum. Even today, the city is a Mecca for the world's top architects, and their angular, avant-garde steel-and-glass structures sit comfortably alongside Gothic churches and dazzling *Modernista* edifices – the hallmark of the city.

It would be easy to spend a week simply paying homage to Barcelona's *Modernista* treasures, in particular those of its most famous son Antoni Gaudí. Throughout the world, people have marvelled at the creations and drawn inspiration from this great master – perhaps it's more than a coincidence that *Gaudí* in Catalan means 'delight'! But the city abounds in countless other sights and attractions to appeal to all tastes, pockets and ages, including some of the finest galleries and museums in Europe. It is also home to La Rambla, one of the world's most famous boulevards. This is the street everyone visits, talks about and tries to photograph or paint. It is more theatre than thoroughfare but it is nonetheless a vital part of the city's makeup – this is where Barcelona's heart beats loudest.

A massive facelift prior to the 1992 Olympics converted the previously provincial, old city into a chic, cosmopolitan metropolis bursting with pride and self-confidence. The transformation of the derelict seafront rejuvenated the city, reminding the Barcelonans of their maritime heyday, and giving rise to the slogan *Barcelona oberta al mar* (Barcelona open to the sea). Now, as Barcelona marches into the 21st century, it is considered the 'style capital of

Europe', exuberant and sophisticated, with world-class shopping, an exceptional cultural scene and a flamboyant nightlife – *la movida*. Remember, this is the European capital that never sleeps. Tonight doesn't usually start until tomorrow!

Today, Barcelona continues to reinvent itself district by district, celebrating its past by restoring its old buildings, while at the same time remaining at the forefront of contemporary culture. It is the richest, fastest growing, most creative and most stylish city in Spain and what's more, its motto is *Barcelona Es Teva* (Barcelona belongs to you).

⬤ *A view of the city from La Sagrada Familia*

When to go

CLIMATE

Barcelona has no low season as there are always things going on. The best time to visit, however, is late spring/early summer, when the weather is warm but not too hot, and the street life is at its most vibrant.

The coldest season is winter, with an average temperature of 10°C (54°F). Snow is rare and days are generally mild but damp, with the occasional day of clear blue skies and bright crisp sunshine.

In spring the average temperature is around 15°C (59°F). These are some of the wettest months but, from late March onwards, the weather starts to warm up. After Easter, outdoor café tables become more popular and by May it is usually warm enough to eat al fresco in the evenings.

During summer, the average temperature is around 25°C (75°F), but it can reach 37°C (99°F) in July and August when the humidity can make the city feel oppressively hot and muggy. Although there is little rain, the occasional sudden violent thunderstorm provides a brief but refreshing respite from the heat.

Early autumn is an ideal time to visit, with generally mild sunny weather. The average autumn temperatures are around 16°C (53°F). By mid-October, the fine weather becomes more intermittent, with frequent heavy rainfalls, and the pavement tables disappear until spring.

● *Gaudí's rippling* trencadis *benches in Parc Güell*

ANNUAL EVENTS

Throughout the year, religious processions, festivals and traditions turn the city of Barcelona into an open-air theatre. Here are some of the highlights.

On New Year's Day (1 January), Barcelonans eat 12 grapes for good luck on the stroke of midnight, in time with the chimes. Four to five days later, the *Reis Mags* (the Wise Men) arrive by boat to tour the city, showering the crowd with sweets. This is also when children traditionally receive their Christmas presents, although naughty children are given only a lump of coal.

In February, the *Carnestoltes* is a week of colourful pre-Lenten parades and carnival events, with fancy dress and fireworks, ending on Ash Wednesday with the symbolic burial of a sardine. Easter is marked by a series of church services and processions throughout the city, while godparents traditionally buy their godchildren a *mona*, a religious sculpture made out of chocolate.

Late spring and summer see a variety of unusual Catalan celebrations. Sant Jordí (St George) on 23 April, in honour of the city's patron saint, is a local alternative to St Valentine's Day, when sweethearts exchange gifts: a rose for the woman and a book for the man. La Rambla becomes a huge outdoor bookshop, and over half of Catalonia's book sales take place on this day. Corpus Christi is marked by parades of giants and dancing *capgrossos* (big heads), and the 18th-century tradition of the *Ou com Balla* (dancing egg), when an empty egg is balanced on the jet of the fountain in the *Catedral* cloisters to symbolise water and birth.

Another unique Catalan festivity is the impressive *Trobada Castellera* in mid-June, with *castell* (human tower) building – spectacular balancing acts with young men standing on each other's shoulders in 'towers' up to nine people high. Gràcia comes alive in the second half of August for its showy *Festa Major*, when each street is in competition for the best decorations and the best programme of entertainment and dancing. It culminates with a massive fireworks display and a *Corre Foc* (fire-running), when devils and dragons run through the streets scattering firecrackers.

The city's grandest fiesta, devoted to *La Mercè* (the Madonna), takes place from 17–24 September and includes four days of dancing, fireworks, *castellar* displays, parades and street parties, climaxing with the *Ball de Gegants*, a dance of costumed 5m-high (16ft) giants from Drassanes to Ciutadella, followed by a *Corre Foc* throughout the town.

The close of the year is marked by numerous Christmas festivities, including a traditional craft fair outside the Catedral (from 13 December) and a large crib in Plaça Sant Jaume. Christmas is celebrated on 24 December, as is the custom throughout Spain, with a special family dinner followed by Midnight Mass.

PUBLIC HOLIDAYS

New Year's Day 1 January

Epiphany 6 January

Good Friday and Easter Monday March/April

May Day 1 May

Whit Monday May/June

St John's Day 24 June

Assumption Day 15 August

Catalan National Day 11 September

La Mercè 24 September

Discovery of Americas 12 October

All Saints' Day 1 November

Constitution Day 6 December

Immaculate Conception 8 December

Christmas Day 25 December

St Stephen's Day 26 December

Gaudí & Modernisme

The *Modernisme* movement – a taste for what is modern – emerged in Barcelona at the turn of the 19th century with the aim of breaking away from the past through new art forms. It was Spain's home-grown interpretation of art nouveau and, thanks to its greatest exponent, Antoni Gaudí, Catalan Modernism had the greatest impact, influencing all forms of European art, architecture, literature and theatre and making Barcelona a veritable open-air museum of *Modernista* style.

● *The dragon's back and saint's cross at Casa Batlló*

No single architect has ever marked a major city quite as comprehensively and spectacularly as Gaudí did here. For many people, Gaudí alone is sufficient reason to visit Barcelona. He designed many of its most charismatic buildings; throughout the city mansions, parks, schools, gateways, lamp-posts and sculptures provide a constant reminder of his genius. His innovative work represents a flamboyant fusion of structure and decoration, giving precedence to use of colour and light within architectural forms. His remarkably organic structures are frequently adorned with his trademark pinnacles, towers and rooftop terraces. Particularly striking are **Casa Milà** (see page 92), with its extraordinary rippling façade devoid of straight lines and right-angled corners, and **Casa Batlló** (see page 90), an imaginative example of the fusion of architecture with the decorative arts of the époque. The green, blue and ochre mosaics of this enigmatic building symbolise the scaly skin of the dragon, its knobbly roof the dragon's back, the balconies represent the skulls and bones of its victims, while the tower shows the St George's cross.

However, Gaudí's most emblematic structure is the still unfinished **Temple Expiatori de la Sagrada Família** (see page 94), the city's iconic church which he spent over 40 years creating, personally going out into the street to raise funds among the passers-by to facilitate its construction. 'The patron of this project is not in a hurry' he once remarked. Tragically, in 1926 he was run over by a tram on the Gran Via and died unrecognised in hospital. When his identity was eventually discovered, Barcelona gave him what was almost a state funeral. His body is fittingly buried in the crypt of the Temple to which he devoted his life.

GAUDÍ'S BARCELONA HIGHLIGHTS
Casa Batlló (see page 90)
Parc Güell (see page 97)
Palau Güell (see page 107)
La Sagrada Família (see page 94)
Casa Milà 'La Pedrera' (see page 92)

History

ORIGINS OF THE CITY

According to legend, Hercules founded Barcelona in 2000BC on his colonial expedition from Africa aboard nine boats: *barça* (boat), *nona* (nine). In fact, it was the Carthaginians who first established a stronghold here around 230BC, swiftly followed by the Romans in the 1st century BC. However, the rise of Barcelona's fortunes coincided with the decline of the Roman Empire and the invasion of the Visigoths in 531. In 878, Wilfred 'The Hairy' founded the independent county of Catalonia. He named himself the first Count of Barcelona, thereby founding a dynastic line that was to rule an increasingly powerful nation for several centuries.

THE MEDIEVAL CITY

During the early Middle Ages, Barcelona flourished during Moorish occupation, until the Christians took Barcelona in 1229 under Catalan King Jaume I. The city became a powerful naval base and trading centre – one of the three most important merchant cities in the Mediterranean, along with Genoa and Venice. The lavish medieval mansions of the old town – former residences of the Counts of Barcelona and the Kings of Catalonia and Aragón – together with such impressive new buildings as the Catedral, Santa Maria del Mar and the Drassanes shipyards, stand as testimony to this golden age. In the 15th century, Catalonia became a self-governing region, and built its own parliament buildings in Barcelona. However, from the 16th to the 18th centuries, as Spain's economic focus turned away from the Mediterranean to the colonisation of the Americas, Barcelona experienced a period of economic decline and, during the Spanish War of Succession, Catalonia lost its autonomous status.

THE CATALAN RENAIXENÇA

During the 18th century, Catalonia began to re-emerge, thanks to a steady growth in agriculture, wine production and shipping. The 19th-century industrial revolution created new prosperity in Barcelona, making it the fastest expanding city in Spain. This also brought about a cultural 'renaissance', as Catalan language and literature began to flourish once more.

Hand-in-hand with the cultural renaissance came the *Modernisme* movement (the Catalan offshoot of art nouveau). Ildefons Cerdà designed the grid-like Eixample district to house the burgeoning middle classes, while *Modernista* architects like Gaudí designed the district's apartment buildings and mansions.

BARCELONA TODAY

The 20th century brought Barcelona new challenges, including the Franco dictatorship, which lasted from the end of the Spanish Civil War until 1975, during which time Catalan national identity was totally repressed. However, just as *Modernisme* emerged at the end of the 19th century as a desire for change and renovation, so the 1992 Olympic Games provided a further boost for the city at the end of the 20th century, and an opportunity to reinvent itself. The transformation of the down-at-heel waterfront was one of the most popular aspects of the city's radical Olympic revamp.

Today, the city goes from strength to strength, renovating and reinventing itself district by district, with La Ribera, El Born and El Raval emerging as newly fashionable quarters. Barcelona keeps its reputation as a forward-looking city at the forefront of design and contemporary culture.

Lifestyle

Barcelonans are fiercely proud of their unique Catalan culture and will repeatedly inform you that Catalonia and its capital city are not Spanish. Indeed they will even try to convince you that Barcelona, not Madrid, is Spain's premier city and, in their eyes, it really is.

⬥ *Al fresco dining in Barceloneta outside Palau del Mar*

Their pride in their city and in their regional culture is manifested in every aspect of daily life – in their cuisine (see page 24) and in their language. Although Barcelona still has two official languages, Catalan and Castilian Spanish, *Català* has more or less taken over as the everyday language.

Even the city's celebrated football team, FC Barça, represents so much more than just a football club. During the Franco era, it was a rallying point for Catalans at matches against their arch-rivals, Real Madrid, and it became the focus of their hatred of central government. At the height of the dictatorship, match results were pre-ordained so that Madrid would win. Still today, whenever they play Real Madrid, all of Spain is gripped, and should Barça win, the streets of Barcelona erupt to the sound of car horns, fireworks and popping *cava* corks.

Barcelonans certainly know how to enjoy themselves, and no month goes by without a festival, a fiesta or a public holiday. But they are also hard-working and prosperous. In a recent survey, Barcelona's economic progress was ranked third among cities of the world. Punctuality is important for meetings, and formal wear is the norm. Business hours are generally 08.00 or 09.00 until 18.00 or 19.00, with a lengthy lunch break between 13.30 and 15.30 or 16.00 to include an afternoon siesta during hotter months.

Barcelonans rarely invite guests into their home. As in many Mediterranean countries, they prefer to socialise in the city's 2,500 bars, cafés and restaurants. Eating is regarded as one of life's great pleasures, and mealtimes are often lengthy gatherings with all the family. And there is no denying that Barcelonans are night owls. The city's intoxicating club scene is among the best (and the latest) in Europe. Here evening begins when most people elsewhere have already gone to bed.

Culture

Barcelona is one of Europe's great cities, thanks mainly to its rich cultural heritage and the dynamism of the contemporary arts and design scene. It is exceptional for the quantity and quality of museums and galleries in proportion to its size – with over 50 to choose from, together with a busy calendar of music and arts events in theatres and concert venues throughout the city, not to mention an impressive range of street artists and entertainers.

Make the informative Museu d'Història de la Ciutat (City History Museum), the lively Museu d'Història de Catalunya (Museum of Catalan History) or the fascinating Museu Marítim (Maritime Museum) your first port of call. Once you have a grasp of the city's colourful history, walks around town are all the more rewarding. If you intend to visit several museums, it is worth getting a *Barcelona Card* (valid for two, three, four or five days), which offers discounts of 10–100% at the city's main museums, together with free travel on public transport (available from tourist offices and participating museums).

The city galleries showcase some dazzling permanent collections of works by three of the prime movers and shakers in Spanish modern art – Pablo Picasso, Joan Miró and Antoni Tàpies. The Museu Nacional d'Art de Catalunya spans several centuries with its remarkable displays, which include one of the world's most important collections of Romanesque art and an impressive selection of Modernist *objets d'art*, while the Museu d'Art Contemporani de Barcelona contains some striking contemporary art. Art aficionados should consider purchasing an *Articket*, a multi-

● *Sculpture at the Fundació Joan Miró*

ticket providing half-price admission to six of the city's foremost art centres: MNAC, Fundació Joan Miró, Fundació Antoni Tàpies, CCCB, Centre Cultural Caixa Catalunya, MACBA and Museu Picasso.

Barcelona also boasts some of the world's finest and most eccentric architecture. Its extraordinary urban landscape resembles a living museum, from the ancient Gothic quarter, built within the Roman city walls – a honey-coloured maze of dark, narrow alleys and charming, hidden squares – to the regimental grid plan of the turn-of-the-century Eixample district, studded with its many eye-catching jewels of *Modernista* architecture, and beyond to the space-age constructions for the 1992 Olympics.

The city is a showcase for the best of Spain's theatrical talent, and is home to such renowned troupes as *Els Comediants*, *La Fura dels Baus*, *Els Joglars* and *El Tricicle*. It is also famed for its wide diversity of musical events from classical music, opera and ballet through jazz, pop and rock, to some of the most innovative music festivals in Europe. In 1999, the city opened the Auditori arts centre (home to the National Catalan Orchestra), with an impressive programme to suit all tastes. In the same year, the city regained its prestigious opera house, the Gran Teatre del Liceu, whose season runs from October until mid-July, with ballet staged during summer months. Another major classical music venue, the Palau de la Música Catalana – a *Modernista* gem – is worth visiting whatever the programme!

One of the most important annual musical events is the 'Grec' Summer Festival, staged at the Teatre Grec on Montjuïc hill – an ambitious open-air programme of theatre, music and dance. Other festivals are devoted to jazz, flamenco and contemporary music.

▶ *Rooftop chimneys at Casa Milà 'La Pedrera'*

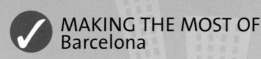

Shopping

As a leading European city of fashion and design, Barcelona offers a wealth of shopping opportunities from designer boutiques to quirky speciality shops, small district markets to glitzy department stores. It offers a unique shopping experience, cleverly fusing tradition and innovation, and its main interior design stores and small, eccentric boutiques make the hunt for gifts and souvenirs here especially enjoyable.

Best buys include clothing, shoes and decorative goods. Look out for local designers Adolfo Dominguez, Antoni Miró, Josep Font and

⬤ *Reflections – the Maremagnum shopping centre at Port Vell*

Lydia Delgado for fashions; Hermenegildo Muxart for footwear; and interior designers, André Ricard, Ricardo Bofil and Javier Mariscal. The latter is one of the trendiest designers in town, famous for creating the ever-popular 'Cobi' mascot for the Olympic games.

Shopaholics should start their spending spree in the Eixample district, where the grid-like streets are lined with chic interior design shops and prestigious fashion emporia. The most exclusive streets are brilliant for window-shopping: Passeig de Gràcia and La Rambla de Catalunya, and along the Avinguda Diagonal between Plaça Joan Carles I and Plaça Francesc Macià.

Old-fashioned arts and crafts shops juxtapose more off-beat boutiques in the intimate streets and alleyways of the Barri Gòtic. Try Carrer Banys Nous for arts and antiques; Carrer Petritxol for home accessories and gift ideas; and Carrer Portal de l'Angel and Carrer Portaferrissa for fashion and shoes.

The newly trendy neighbouring districts of La Ribera and El Born contain a myriad of tiny craft workshops, jewellers and designer boutiques, as well as some superb art galleries in the streets around Museu Picasso. El Corte Inglés is the city's foremost department store, with several different locations (including Plaça Catalunya and Avinguda Diagonal), and the waterfront also attracts shoppers to the Maremagnum shopping centre.

Larger shops tend to open 09.00 to 21.00 Monday–Saturday. Smaller shops close during the siesta (13.00–16.30), close early on Saturdays and frequently stay shut on Mondays. Some shopping centres (including Maremagnum) also open on Sundays, and food shops and markets generally open early in the morning. There are covered markets in every district of the city, but the most famous, La Boqueria, is centrally placed and one of the best places to stock up on picnic supplies.

Eating & drinking

Don't let Barcelona's dazzling cultural scene divert you from its culinary excellence. The city boasts a huge culture of eating, drinking and conversation, with lengthy lunches and late night

● *Dishing up paella in La Barceloneta*

dining, and a bewildering choice of eateries from spacious designer brasseries to tiny neighbourhood tapas bars.

WHEN TO EAT

Barcelonans enjoy good food and often eat out. It is customary in Catalonia to eat late, with lunch served typically from 14.00 to 16.00, aperitifs and tapas in the early evening, then dinner from 21.00 to midnight or later. Many cafés and bars remain open from early morning until late at night. It is advisable to book in most restaurants, especially at weekends. Most offer a fixed price *menu del dìa* (menu of the day), which is usually good value but restrictive. The *à la carte* menus generally offer some of the more unusual dishes and regional specialities. Prices on the menu include VAT (*IVA*), unless stated, and it is customary to tip by rounding up the bill after a meal, or to add on 5–10% if you are feeling generous.

WHAT TO EAT

There are restaurants to suit all tastes, budgets and occasions, with specialities from all over the world. There is no such thing as Spanish 'national cuisine' but it is possible to taste various local styles, including Galician and Basque. The majority of restaurants serve the regional cuisine, *la cuina Catalana* – a Mediterranean style of cooking, with bold, sun-drenched flavours.

PRICE RATING
The restaurant price guides indicate the approximate cost of a three-course meal for one person, excluding drinks, at the time of writing.
£ up to €25; ££ between €25 and €50; £££ above €50

Traditional Catalan dishes lean heavily on olive oil, tomatoes, garlic, peppers, aubergines, courgettes and herbs which, when blended, form *samfaina*, a delicious and popular sauce served with many meat and fish dishes. Other common sauces include *romesco* (nuts, tomatoes and spicy red pepper) and *allioli* (a strong, garlicky mayonnaise). Pork is the mainstay of the Catalan diet, although chicken, lamb, duck, beef and game dishes are popular too. Meats are often combined with fruit in such delicacies as *pollastre amb pera* (chicken with pears) and *conill amb prunes* (rabbit with prunes). Seafood is hugely popular too, from simply grilled sardines to a hearty *sarsuela* (seafood stew). Try the local variant on *paella*, called *fideuà* (using pasta rather than rice) and the eye-catching shellfish platters. Catalan cuisine is unique within Spain for mixing fish and meat together to create such exotic dishes as *sepia amb mandonguilles* (squid with meatballs) and *mar i cel* (sea and heaven) – a combination of sausages, rabbit, prawns and fish.

The best-known Catalan dessert is *crèma catalana* (*crème brûlée*). Look out also for *mel i mató* (curd cheese with honey); *postre de músic*, a delicious spiced fruit cake; and *cocas* (pastries sprinkled with sugar and pine nuts).

Wash your meal down with some excellent locally produced Penedès wines (see page 133) and *cavas* (sparkling wines).

TAPAS

Tapas bars abound throughout the city, serving savoury snacks with a pre-meal drink to *tapar el apetito* (to put a lid on the appetite). If you are overwhelmed by the mouth-watering counter displays, simply point to one or two tempting dishes or order a *tapa combinada* – a bit of everything!

WHERE TO EAT

The Barri Gòtic and Gràcia contain a variety of small, atmospheric restaurants that are generally reasonably priced. Eateries on La Rambla tend to be over-priced and touristic. The Eixample is slightly more upmarket, and contains some excellent tapas bars, and there are plenty of intimate, candlelit bistros and fashionable brasseries to be found in La Ribera, El Born and, increasingly, in El Raval. For seafood, head to the Olympic Port or to the atmospheric fishing district of La Barceloneta.

USEFUL DINING PHRASES IN SPANISH
(See also pages 154–5)

I would like a table for ... people
Quisiera una mesa para ... personas
Keyseeyera oona mesa para ... personas

May I have the bill, please?
¿Podría traerme la cuenta
por favor?
*¿Pordreea trayerme la cwenta
por farbor?*

Waiter/waitress!
¡Camarero/Camarera!
¡Camareroe/Camarera!

Could I have it well-cooked/medium/rare please?
¿Por favor, la carne bien cocida/al punto/roja?
¿Porr fabor, la kahrrne beeyen kotheeda/al poontoh/roha?

I am a vegetarian. Does this contain meat?
Soy vegetariano. ¿Tiene carne este plato?
Soy begetahreeahnoh. ¿Teeyene carneh esteh plahtoh?

Entertainment & nightlife

Barcelona is a city of night owls, and the vibrant club scene is among the best in Europe. There is plenty to choose from every night, and weekends here begin on Thursday. A typical evening begins around 20.30 with tapas and aperitifs in a local bar, followed by a leisurely dinner around 22.30. The usual starting time for opera, ballet and concerts is around 21.00, or 22.00 for theatre. After midnight, music bars become crowded. Around 03.00 the clubs and discos fill up and the famous Barcelonan night movement – *la movida* – sweeps across the city until dawn. The main nightlife areas are La Ribera, with its myriad small bars, and the chic nightspots of L'Eixample. However, the Barri Gòtic and El Raval are also lively and some of the top bars and clubs are further afield – on Montjuïc hill and the lower slopes of Tibidabo.

The city's flamboyant club scene caters to all tastes, although house and electronic beats take centre stage at present. Many of the clubs are on the European circuit for celebrated DJs and live bands, and there is even an annual Sonar festival of experimental music in June, attracting all the big names in digital sound. During summer, the beachfront clubs often have outdoor dancing, and some inland clubs have fantastic garden dance-terraces, some with swimming pools. There are also numerous Latin clubs featuring salsa, meringue and samba beats. Entry to the top clubs is not cheap, so look out for free entry passes at various bars around the city centre or discount flyers which are sometimes handed out on La Rambla at night. The city also boasts numerous live music venues, ranging from vast rock and pop arenas to traditional flamenco clubs and mellow, intimate jazz bars featuring artists from all over the world.

On the cultural front, there is a wide-ranging programme of classical music, ballet and dance, staged in such impressive venues as the beautiful *Modernista* Palau de la Música Catalana and the Gran Teatre del Liceu, one of the world's largest and most celebrated opera houses. Throughout the year, recitals are staged in churches,

⬤ *A tempting display at one of Barcelona's many tapas bars*

museums and monasteries, and during summer months in some of the city parks, including Ciutadella Park, Parc Güell and the Teatre Grec on Montjuïc hill, which stages an open-air summer festival of theatre, music and dance. Barcelona's theatre programme is unlikely to appeal to visitors, unless you speak Catalan or Spanish, in which case there is the full spectrum from classical to avant-garde on offer. Cinema, however, is a different matter, with most screenings in the original version with subtitles.

Tickets are best purchased from the relevant box office at each venue. Alternatively, you can book by phone or via the Internet and collect the tickets at the venue, from Servi-Caixa (① 902 332 211 ⑩ www.serviticket.com) and Tel-Entrada (① 902 101 212 ⑩ www.telentrada.com) – operated by two of the city's largest

BARS & CLUBS

The best source of local entertainment listings is a magazine called *Guía del Ocio* (www.guiadelociobcn.es), available from newsstands. It previews cinema, theatre, music and nightlife for the week, together with extensive sections on bars, restaurants and the city's thriving gay scene. *See Barcelona* (⑩ www. seebarcelona.com) produces a free quarterly listings guide in English, which is available in tourist information offices and some hotels, shops and restaurants. The local paper, *La Vanguardia* (⑩ www.lavanguardia.es) also has an arts and entertainments page. The leaflet *Informatíu Musical*, available free from tourist offices, record shops and concert venues, is an excellent source of concert and recital information. There is also a cultural information desk at Palau de la Virreina (③ La Rambla 99 ① 933 017 775).

savings banks, La Caixa and Caixa Catalunya. Servi-Caixa has special machines next to La Caixa's ATMs, which print out the tickets; Tel-entrada is operated out of larger branches of Caixa Catalunya, and at a dedicated desk in the Plaça de Catalunya tourist office.

⬥ *Street sculpture – Barcelona Head by Roy Lichtenstein*

Sport & relaxation

SPECTATOR SPORTS

Barcelonans are football crazy and no visit to the city is complete for sports fans without a visit to Camp Nou, home to FC Barcelona (ⓦ www.fcbarcelona.com) and one of the great shrines of world football. Other celebrated city teams include the 'Barcelona Dragons' (ⓦ www.fcbarcelonaweb.com/dragons/), who play in the World League of American Football on Sundays from April to June at the Estadi Olímpic; Joventut (ⓦ www.penya.com), the top basketball team, which plays league games on Sunday evenings and European and Spanish Cup matches midweek from September to May in the arena at the Pabellón Olímpico (Olympic Pavilion) at Badalona, just outside the city; and FC Barcelona Pista de Gel, the city's sole ice hockey team, which plays at the ice rink on Montjuïc hill.

Bullfighting was popular until 2004, when the city council took an historic vote and declared Barcelona an anti-bullfighting city. Both the city's bullrings were forced into disuse, although there is still an interesting museum about the sport (Museu Tauri) at Carrer Muntaner 24.

HOW TO GET TICKETS
Tickets for all major sporting events are available directly from each venue, or via the Internet at www.serviticket.com or www.barcelona-ticket-office.com.

PARTICIPATORY SPORTS

Following its hugely successful Olympic Games in 1992, Barcelona's sporting facilities are second to none.

For racket sports, the Centre Municipal de Tennis Vall d'Hebron (🄰 Passeig de la Vall d'Hebron 178 🄣 934 276 500), built for the Olympics, has clay courts open to the public, while Squash Barcelona (Avinguda del Doctor Maranón 17 🄣 933 340 258) is the city's largest squash complex with 14 squash courts and two racket-ball courts. Telephone in advance to book a court.

For water sports, several clubs offer weekend courses in sailing and windsurfing. Contact the Centre Municipal de Vella, Port Olímpic (🄣 932 257 940) for details. If you don't fancy swimming in the sea, the Olympic Piscina Bernat Picornell (Avenida de l'Estadi 30–40) is one of several swimming pools open to the public.

For further details of participatory sports, contact the sports information service (🄰 Avenida de l'Estadi 30–40 🄣 934 023 000) for details of city-run sports centres and facilities.

🄾 Aerial view of the Olympic port

Accommodation

Barcelona offers a wide range of hotels from cool, contemporary boutique hotels and deluxe belle époque palace hotels, to simple B&Bs and hostels. The luxury hotels are generally extremely expensive and it can be difficult to find quality budget accommodation even during winter months.

Many of the more affordable hotels are located in the atmospheric Barri Gòtic. Those on or near La Rambla may be noisy at night. The Eixample offers a wider range of hotels, especially in the mid-range price bracket, but these often sacrifice character for functionality. There are no campsites in the city but there are plenty of youth hostels for budget travellers, and many are centrally located. Apartment hotels are a good bet for extended stays, especially if you're travelling as a family.

Whatever your accommodation, early booking is essential and remember that breakfasts are usually additional and all hotel bills are subject to 7% VAT on top of the basic price. There is usually also a charge for secure hotel car parking. It is virtually impossible to find a hotel off the street so, if you haven't booked in advance, try the hotel-finding agency Ultramar Express (❶ 934 914 463 ❷ 08.00–22.00) in Sants railway station or the main tourist office (❶ 933 043 232 ❷ 09.00–21.00) in Plaça de Catalunya.

PRICE RATINGS
The ratings below (unrelated to the official star system) indicate the approximate cost of a room for two people for one night (excluding VAT and breakfast):
£ up to €100; ££ €100–199; £££ over €200

HOTELS

Banys Orientals £ The ultimate in urban chic, located at the heart of the fashionable El Born district and surprisingly affordable. ⓐ Carrer Argenteria 37 ⓣ 932 866 460 ⓦ www.hotelbanysorientals.com ⓜ Metro: Jaume I

Gaudí £ A modern 3-star hotel opposite Gaudí's Palau Güell. Excellent value. ⓐ Carrer Nou de la Rambla 12 ⓣ 933 179 032 ⓜ Metro: Drassanes or Liceu

Jardí £ A popular small hotel on one of the Barri Gòtic's most atmospheric squares. ⓐ Plaça Sant Josep Oriol 1 ⓣ 933 015 900 ⓜ Metro: Liceu

Méson de Castilla £ A family-run hotel with characterful Castillian-style rooms, near MACBA and the CCCB. ⓐ Carrer Valldonzella 5 ⓣ 933 182 182 ⓜ Metro: Universitat

Rialto £ A comfortable hotel in the Barri Gòtic, with stylish Catalan furnishings. ⓐ Carrer Ferran 42 ⓣ 933 185 212 ⓦ www.gargallo-hotels.com ⓜ Metro: Jaume I

Sagrada Família £ A tiny B&B for those seeking home comforts. ⓐ Carrer Nápols 266 ⓣ 933 174 342 ⓦ www.sagradafamilia-bedandbreakfast.com ⓜ Metro: Sagrada Família

Colón ££ Cosy old-fashioned hotel opposite the cathedral – an excellent choice for families. ⓐ Avenida de la Catedral 7 ⓣ 938 450 636 ⓦ www.hotelcolon.es ⓜ Jaume I or Urquinaona

Condes de Barcelona ££ Elegant hotel at the heart of the main shopping district, combining *Modernista* architecture with avant-garde décor. ⓐ Passeig de Gràcia ⓣ 934 450 000 ⓦ www.condesdebarcelona.com ⓜ Metro: Diagonal

Duques de Bergara ££ A traditional-style 4-star hotel, with beautiful *Modernista* architecture and fittings. ⓐ Carrer Bergara 11 ⓣ 933 015 151 ⓦ www.hotels-catalonia.es ⓜ Metro: Catalunya

Neri ££ An intimate boutique hotel with state-of-the-art amenities within a characterful 18th-century palace in the Barri Gòtic.
ⓐ Carrer Sant Sever 5 ⓣ 933 040 655 ⓦ www.hotelneri.com
Ⓜ Metro: Jaume I or Liceu

Arts £££ One of the most fashionable hotels, with high-tech facilities and spa, beside the sea in one of Spain's tallest buildings.
ⓐ Carrer de la Marina 19–21 ⓣ 932 211 000 ⓦ www.harts.es
Ⓜ Metro: Ciutadella or Vila Olímpica

Claris £££ Unabashed luxury amid sleek marble, glass and modern artworks in the Eixample district. ⓐ Carrer Pau Claris 150 ⓣ 934 876 262 ⓦ www.derbyhotels.es Ⓜ Metro: Passeig de Gràcia

La Florida £££ The ultimate romantic getaway – a 5-star historic hotel with post-modern interiors on Mont Tibidabo, with sensational spa, edgeless indoor-outdoor swimming pool and gardens overlooking the city. ⓐ Carretera Vallvidrera al Tibidabo 83–93 ⓣ 932 593 000 ⓦ www.hotellaflorida.com

Omm £££ Cutting-edge boutique hotel with minimalist interiors, relaxation centre, nightclub, rooftop pool and celebrated restaurant.
ⓐ Carrer Rossello 265 ⓣ 934 454 000 ⓦ www.hotelomm.es
Ⓜ Metro: Diagonal

Ritz £££ One of Barcelona's top traditional-style hotels, combining old-world charm with top-class service. ⓐ Gran Via 668 ⓣ 933 185 200 ⓦ www.ritzbcn.com Ⓜ Metro: Passeig de Gràcia

YOUTH HOSTELS

Alberg Kabul £ This popular backpackers hostel in lively Plaça Reial has a superb party atmosphere. ⓐ Plaça Reial 17 ⓣ 933 185 190
ⓦ www.kabul.es Ⓜ Metro: Liceu

Centric Point £ One of the newest youth hostels in town, with broadband Internet access, bar, satellite TV and free breakfast.

ⓐ Passeig de Gràcia 33 ① 932 312 045
ⓦ www.centricpointhostel.com Ⓝ Metro: Passeig de Gràcia

🔺 *The striking Hotel Arts enjoys a wonderful beachside location*

THE BEST OF BARCELONA

There's plenty in Barcelona to fill even a long city break but if you have only a few days to spare then here's our list of sights and experiences you should really try not to miss.

TOP 10 ATTRACTIONS

- **La Sagrada Família** This eccentric cathedral is a marvel of *Modernista* architecture and Gaudí's most celebrated creation (see page 94).

- **Museu Picasso** The world's greatest collection of artworks by Pablo Picasso (see page 80).

- **Museu Nacional d'Art de Catalunya** (MNAC) One thousand years of Catalan art under one roof (see page 112).

- **Catedral** A magnificent example of Catalan Gothic style, and one of the finest cathedrals in Spain (see page 64).

- **Parc Güell** Gaudí's flamboyant hilltop park is an extraordinary piece of landscape design (see page 97).

- **Fundació Joan Miró** A dazzling gallery devoted to one of Barcelona's finest artists (see page 111).

- **La Rambla** The most famous boulevard in Spain and the hub of city life for locals and visitors alike (see page 58).

- **El Born and Santa Maria del Mar** The city's 'seaside cathedral' is striking in its simplicity. You'll find it in the trendy El Born area of the city (see pages 76 & 78).

- **Palau de la Música Catalana** One of the city's greatest *Modernista* masterpieces (see page 80).

- **Camp Nou** Home of FC Barcelona. If you can't get a ticket for a match, at least visit the museum and take a tour of the stadium (see page 120).

🔻 *Detail of Gaudí's* trencadís *technique*

Here's a quick guide to seeing the best of Barcelona, depending on the time you have available.

HALF-DAY: BARCELONA IN A HURRY

If you have only a few hours, start your visit promenading with locals along the city's most famous boulevard, La Rambla. Then explore the dark atmospheric streets and enchanting squares of the Barri Gòtic. Art lovers should also visit the remarkable collections of Museu Picasso in the neighbouring La Ribera district.

1 DAY: TIME TO SEE A LITTLE MORE

Having completed the half-day itinerary, you are now at the heart of the fashionable La Ribera district with its myriad hip fashion

● *Check out the Museu Nacional d'Art de Catalunya (MNAC)*

boutiques, galleries and design shops, so add some shopping to your day. Alternatively, visit the beautiful church of Santa Maria del Mar or take in a museum. The Museu d'Història de Catalunya is especially interesting. For dinner, head back to the trendy bars and bistros of La Ribera or enjoy more traditional dishes and some of the city's finest seafood in the Barceloneta district.

2–3 DAYS: SHORT CITY-BREAK

These extra days provide plenty of time to explore the city's museums and spectacular *Modernista* architecture. The Eixample district contains many of the most famous buildings. Shopaholics will also enjoy Passeig de Gràcia – the Champs Elysées of Barcelona – for its exclusive shops and designer boutiques. There are also some excellent tapas bars here for a light lunch, before heading off to admire Gaudí's most celebrated sights – La Sagrada Família and Parc Güell.

Or visit Montjuïc hill and spend the day marvelling at such major museums as the Museu Nacional d'Art de Catalunya (MNAC) and the Fundació Joan Miró. Return to the old town for dinner in the Barri Gòtic. You may also have time to explore the rejuvenated waterfront, including Port Vell with its impressive Maremagnum shopping complex and the ancient royal shipyards of the Museu Marítim.

LONGER: ENJOYING BARCELONA TO THE FULL

A longer stay enables you to soak up the café culture of the old town, to top up your tan on the beaches and to visit some of the outlying districts of town, including Pedralbes with its monastery and museums, and Mont Tibidabo in the Collserola hills. For out of town trips, see page 130.

Something for nothing

Barcelona is an excellent city for budget travellers, with plenty of free sights and attractions.

For a taste of Barcelona's history, stroll the narrow maze of alleyways of the medieval Barri Gòtic district; explore the 'open-air museum' district of L'Eixample to marvel at the *Modernista* architecture of the early 20th century; and visit Montjuïc hill to admire the high-tech sporting facilities of the 1992 Olympics. Some museums offer free entry once a month (including Museu Picasso, Museu Frederic Marès and Museu d'Història de Catalunya on the first Sunday of the month, and MNAC on the first Thursday of the month). In many ways, the entire city resembles a giant outdoor gallery, with over 400 open-air monuments and sculptures to enjoy.

Shopping fanatics on a budget can enjoy some of the world's finest window-shopping, especially on Passeig de Gràcia, the Diagonal and in La Ribera and El Born. There are also several worthwhile markets to browse, including an antiques market in Plaça del Pi on Thursdays; the weekend art market in Plaça Sant Josep Oriol; the Sunday coin and stamp market in Plaça Reial; and the sensational daily food market of La Boqueria.

Alternatively, escape the bustle of downtown Barcelona and walk in the Collserola hills or head for the city's beautiful parks. Relax in tranquil Parc de la Ciutadella or admire the sweeping city vistas and unusual sculptures of Gaudí's Parc Güell. Many parks contain playgrounds and attractions for children including Parc de l'Espanya Industrial with its giant dragon slide and a small boating-lake, and Park del Laberint with a fun topiary maze. The city squares are also great places to sit and watch the world go by: feed the pigeons in Plaça de Catalunya; listen to the buskers in Plaça de Sant Jaume

Oriel; and watch the *sardana* dancers perform in Plaça de la Seu or Plaça Sant Jaume on Sunday mornings. It's also fun to people-watch on La Rambla, and enjoy the lively street entertainment every few paces ranging from buskers and magicians to human statues. And on lazy summer days, where better to while away the hours than on Barcelona's fine, sandy beaches?

⬤ *Take a siesta in Parc Güell*

When it rains

It rarely rains in Barcelona. On average the city has 300 days of sunshine each year and the tendency is for brief showers rather than day-long downpours. It is more likely that you will want to spend time indoors to get out of the heat than the rain. However,

● *Escape the elements in the Museu Tauri, the bullfighting museum*

come rain or shine, there are plenty of indoor activities to keep
you amused.

There are over 50 museums and galleries catering for all ages
and interests from highbrow modern art to football. Immerse
yourself in history at the Museu d'Història de la Ciutat or the Museu
Marítim; visit one of numerous art galleries, including Museu
Picasso, Fundació Joan Miró, the Museu Nacional d'Art de Catalunya
and the Museu d'Art Contemporani de Barcelona; or seek refuge
from the elements in the Catedral, the Basílica de Santa Maria del
Mar or the Monestir de Pedralbes. Children especially enjoy the
underwater world at L'Aquàrium; the state-of-the-art IMAX cinema
at Port Vell; and Cosmocaixa, the new hands-on science museum
and planetarium on the lower slopes of Tibidabo.

Barcelona's shopping ranks among the best in the world, and
there are several large department stores and shopping centres to
occupy any keen shopper for hours, including El Corte Inglés, Spain's
main department store, with branches throughout the city;
Maremagnum at Port Vell; and a number of exclusive shopping
malls off Passeig de Gràcia.

If that sounds too energetic, relax at a beauty spa. The Six Senses
Spa at Hotel Arts and the ZenZone Spa at the Gran Hotel La Florida
offer the ultimate in pampering. Or join locals in one of the
numerous bars and cafés. Take your pick of refreshment in spacious
trendy 'design-bars'; *xampanyerías* (champagne bars); cosy old-
fashioned bodegas, serving wine from the barrel; traditional tapas
bars; and *cervecerias* (beer bars). Or simply master the Barcelonan
art of coffee drinking in one of the characterful locals' cafés: try *cafè
amb llet* (a large milky coffee) for breakfast; a *tallat* (a small coffee
with a dash of milk) or a *cafè sol* (espresso) at midday; and a *carajillo*
(a *sol* with a shot of brandy) after dinner.

On arrival

ARRIVING
By air

Barcelona's airport, El Prat de Llobregat (☎ 932 983 838
ⓦ www.aena.es ⓔ bcninformacion@aena.es) is situated 12 km
(8 miles) southwest of Barcelona. It has excellent facilities within
its three terminals, including numerous shops, restaurants, bars,
tourist information offices, bureaux de change, banks and ATMs,
post office, left luggage, a chemist and car hire facilities. There are
also 24-hour medical facilities in the Bloque Técnico (Technical
Block). There is no dedicated business centre but there are VIP
lounges in Terminals A and B, and a meeting room, which is
available for hire in Terminal B (☎ 932 983 815).

The best way to reach the city centre from the airport is by taxi. This takes around 20–30 minutes but it is the most expensive option. There is also a regular *Aerobus* bus service every 15 minutes (06.00–24.00) from the airport to Plaça de Catalunya, via Plaça d'Espanya, Gran Via de les Corts Catalanes and Plaça de la Universitat. Tickets are available from the driver and the journey takes about 30 minutes. At rush hour, the regular rail service (06.00–22.00) is a quicker option. It runs to Estació Sants, Urquinaona, Arc de Triomf and Clot-Aragó, all of which connect with the metro.

By rail

The city's main railway station, Estació Sants (ⓐ Plaça del Països Catalans ❶ 934 956 215), is the main arrival point from both national

● *Barcelona's bustling Plaça d'Espanya*

Barcelona

and international destinations, which also connects with the metro network. Facilities include tourist information, hotel information, bank, restaurants, shops, first-aid and left luggage lockers. Other major railway stations in the city include Estació de França (🅐 Avenida Marqués de l'Argentera), near Barceloneta metro station, and Estació Passeig de Gràcia, near Plaça de Catalunya.

By road

Eurolines (🅣 902 405 040 🅦 www.eurolines.es) provide coach links with most major Spanish cities, and arrive into Estació del Nord (🅐 Avinguda Vilanova 🅣 902 260 606). Coaches from foreign cities generally arrive into Estació Autobuses de Sants (🅐 Carrer Viriato 🅣 934 904 000), beside the main Sants railway station.

IF YOU GET LOST, TRY SOME SPANISH
(See also pages 154–5)

Excuse me, do you speak English?
Perdone, ¿habla usted inglés?
Perdoene, ¿ahbla oosteth eengless?

Excuse me, is this the right way to the old town/the city centre/the tourist office/the station/the bus station?
Perdone, ¿por aquí se va a el casco antiguo/al centro de la ciudad/oficina de turísmo/la estación de trenes/estación de autobuses?
Perdoneh, ¿porr akee seh bah ah el kasko antigwo/al thentroe de la theeoodath/offeetheena deh toorismoe/la estatheeon de trenes/estatheeon dey awtoebooses?

If you are driving, the A7 motorway is the main route to Barcelona from France, while the A2 joins Zaragoza to the west, with connections from Madrid. The Barcelona ring road makes it easy to approach the city centre from all directions but, once in the centre, driving can be quite daunting with fast multi-lane avenues and complicated one-way systems. Parking can also be difficult and car parks are expensive. Your best bet is to find a space marked in blue with a *Zona Blava* (Blue Zone) sign and to purchase a ticket from a nearby parking meter. Parking costs around €1–3 per hour. If you park illegally, your car may be towed away.

FINDING YOUR FEET

On first impression, Barcelona appears to be a bustling Mediterranean city but the pace of life here is surprisingly relaxed. The people are laid-back and friendly. As with most major cities, there are incidents of petty crime, so it is advisable to take commonsense precautions (see page 145).

ORIENTATION

It is easy to find your way around Barcelona as the city is divided into districts, each with its own distinctive characteristics, and the public transport system is easy to use and very efficient. You may get lost in the labyrinth of narrow streets and dark alleys of the Barri Gòtic and La Ribera, but that is half the fun. Arm yourself with a good map! L'Eixample can be a little confusing at times as it is built on a grid system with extremely long avenues and identical-looking blocks of buildings. Should you get lost, there are certain unmissable landmarks, such as the sea, Montjuïc hill and Mont Tibidabo, to help you get your bearings.

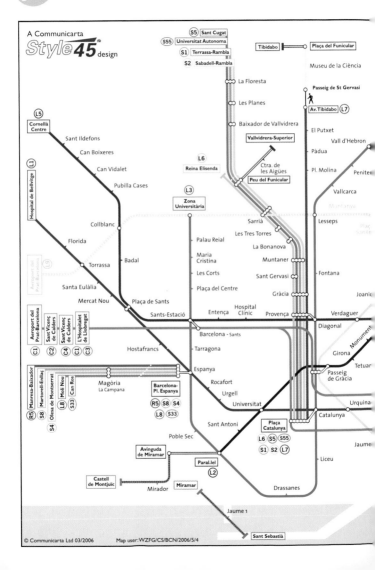

GETTING AROUND

The metro network, operated by TMB (ⓦ www.tmb.net) is the most efficient means of transport in the city. It is easy to use, with just five lines, each identified by a number and a colour, and the direction is indicated by the end-station of each line. The metro runs 05.00–24.00 Mon–Thur, 05.00–02.00 Fri–Sat and 06.00–24.00 Sun.

For the suburbs and surrounding areas there are regional rail lines run by the Ferrocarrils de la Generalitat de Catalunya – FGC (ⓦ www.fgc.es) and RENFE. The FGC line is fully integrated into the metro system and runs 05.45–24.00 Mon–Thur, 05.50–02.15 Fri–Sat and 05.50–24.00 Sun. The main station for the regional trains is at Plaça de Catalunya. Tickets are available for purchase at ticket offices and automatic vending machines at each station. Remember to validate your ticket in a machine on the platform before boarding.

There is also an extensive bus network, operated by TMB from 06.30–22.00, with most services passing through Plaça de Catalunya, Plaça Urquinaona or Plaça de la Universitat. Purchase your tickets from the driver and validate it in the machines on the buses. The city's 16 night-bus routes, which run approximately every half-hour from 23.00–04.00, require separate tickets.

If you intend to use the bus and metro frequently, consider one of the special multi-ride tickets available from metro ticket offices, automatic vending machines and FGC railway stations. These include the T-10 for 10 journeys; a T-dia one-day pass and also special tourist passes, valid for two, three, four and five days, which cover all transport in the city, including the journey to and from the airport.

The Bus Turístic is an easy way to get around with 42 hop-on-hop-off stops. There are two main routes which embrace all the main city sights, starting from Plaça de Catalunya and lasting about 2 hours. The buses run every 6–20 minutes, depending on the season, daily from 09.00–19.00 (until 20.00 Apr–Oct), except 25 Dec and 1 Jan. Tickets are available for one or two days and cost €18 and €22 respectively.

Look out also for the TombBús – a special shopping service which runs every 7 minutes on weekdays (07.30–21.58) and every 15 minutes on Saturdays (09.30–21.45) between Plaça de Catalunya and Plaça Pius XII.

⬥ *Street art on Montjuïc hill*

Other modes of public transport include the funicular railway up Montjuïc from Avinguda Paral.lel to Avinguda Miramar from 09.00–20.00 (22.00 in summer), with a cable car leading up to Montjuïc castle from 11.00–19.15; a second cable car runs from Barceloneta to Montjuïc, 10.30–19.00 (Mar to mid-June), 10.30–20.00 (mid-June to mid-Sept), 10.30–19.00 (mid-Sept to mid-Oct) and 10.30–17.30 (mid-Oct to Feb); the Golondrinas pleasure boat tours (see page 74); the ancient *Tramvia Blau* (Blue Tram) from FGC Avinguda Tibidabo to Plaça Doctor Andreu (see page 124); and the Funicular de Tibidabo (see page 124).

Black-and-yellow taxis can be hailed in the street or booked in advance, but they are an expensive option. Reliable companies include Radio Taxi (❶ 933 033 033) and Servitaxi (❶ 933 300 300). Alternatively, hire a bicycle from Un Coxte Menys (❷ Carrer Esparteria 3 ❶ 932 682 105) at around €5 an hour or €15 a day.

CAR HIRE

The excellent public transport system in Barcelona makes driving unnecessary in the city. It is only worthwhile hiring a car if you are planning to explore Catalonia. There are several car rental companies at the airport, although pre-booking with your airline's affiliates should secure you reduced rates.

Avis ❷ Terminals B & C ❶ 932 983 601 ❿ www.avis.es
Europcar ❷ Terminals B & C ❶ 932 983 300 ❿ www.europcar.es
Hertz ❷ Terminals B & C ❶ 932 983 637 ❿ www.hertz.es
National Atesa ❶ Terminals B & C ❶ 932 983 433 ❿ www.atesa.es

❿ *La Barceloneta waterfront*

THE CITY OF
Barcelona

La Rambla & Barri Gòtic

Sooner or later, all visitors to Barcelona find themselves strolling with locals on La Rambla, Spain's most famous and well-trodden boulevard, abuzz with market stalls, artists and street entertainers. It leads through the heart of the old city down to the port. Just off La Rambla, the Barri Gòtic (Gothic Quarter) is Barcelona's oldest district, brimming with atmospheric streets, alleyways and hidden squares, and flanked by countless buildings of historical interest. The Barri Gòtic is something of a misnomer as the district combines its splendid Gothic architecture with Roman, Romanesque and Renaissance elements, making it a fascinating area to explore.

SIGHTS & ATTRACTIONS

La Rambla

La Rambla is among the Mediterranean's most celebrated boulevards, and the pride of Barcelona. This magnificent 18th-century tree-lined promenade – with its cafés, buskers, newsstands, street artists and bustling crowds of locals and tourists – is where the city's heart beats loudest. Along the route, there are various distinctive sections each with their own characteristics, from the portrait painters of the Rambla de Santa Mònica to the birdcages of the Rambla dels Ocells and the flower stalls of Rambla de les Flors. Other significant landmarks include the Mercat de la Boqueria (see page 68), Barcelona's central market, and the Gran Teatre del Liceu, the city's celebrated opera house (see page 65). Don't forget to drink from the famous iron fountain of La Rambla de Canaletes (at the northernmost end) – according to legend, just one sip ensures your return to the city.
ⓐ La Rambla ⓝ Metro: Catalunya, Liceu or Drassanes

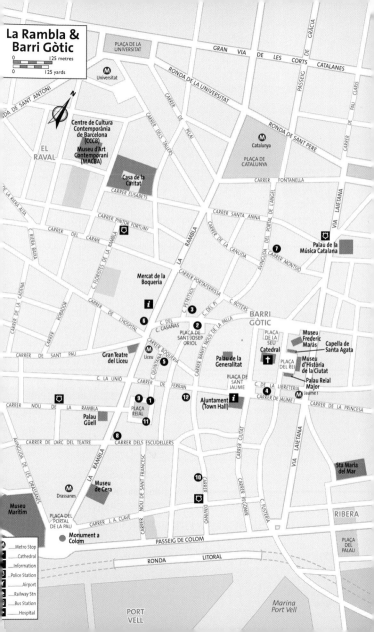

La Rambla & Barri Gòtic

0 — 125 metres
0 — 125 yards

EL RAVAL

BARRI GÒTIC

RIBERA

Centre de Cultura
Contemporània
de Barcelona
(CCCB)

Museu d'Art
Contemporani
(MACBA)

Casa de la
Caritat

Mercat de la
Boqueria

Gran Teatre
del Liceu

Palau
Güell

Museu de Cera

Museu Marítim

Monument a
Colom

Catedral

Palau de la
Generalitat

Ajuntament
(Town Hall)

Museu Frederic
Marès

Capella de
Santa Agata

Museu
d'Història
de la Ciutat

Palau Reial
Major

Palau de la
Música Catalana

Sta Maria
del Mar

**PLAÇA DE LA
UNIVERSITAT**

**PLAÇA DE
CATALUNYA**

**PLAÇA DE
SANT JOSEP
ORIOL**

**PLAÇA DE
SANT JAUME**

**PLAÇA
REIAL**

**PLAÇA DE
LA SEU**

**PLAÇA
DEL REI**

**PLAÇA DEL
PORTAL
DE LA PAU**

**PLAÇA
DEL
PALAU**

**PORT
VELL**

**Marina
Port Vell**

Streets and features

GRAN VIA DE LES CORTS CATALANES
RONDA DE LA UNIVERSITAT
RONDA DE SANT PERE
CARRER FONTANELLA
CARRER SANTA ANNA
RONDA DE SANT ANTONI
CARRER DELS TALLERS
CARRER DE PELAI
CARRER ELISABETS
CARRER PINTOR FORTUNY
CARRER DEL CARME
CARRER DE LA CANUDA
CARRER PORTAFERRISSA
C. PETRITXOL
CARRER DE L'HOSPITAL
CARRER DE SANT PAU
C. DE LA UNIÓ
CARRER DE FERRAN
CARRER DELS ESCUDELLERS
CARRER DE L'ARC DEL TEATRE
CARRER J. A. CLAVÉ
PASSEIG DE COLOM
RONDA LITORAL
CARRER DE JAUME I
CARRER DE LA PRINCESA
VIA LAIETANA
AVINGUDA DEL PORTAL DE L'ANGEL
PASSEIG DE GRACIA
CARRER DE PAU CLARIS
LA RAMBLA

Legend

- Metro Stop
- Cathedral
- Information
- Police Station
- Airport
- Railway Stn
- Bus Station
- Hospital

WHAT'S IN A NAME

The name 'Rambla' is derived from *ramla* (Arabic for 'torrent'), named after the sandy stream bed here which ran parallel with the medieval city walls, carrying rainwater down to the sea. Dry during summer months, this route soon became the main link to the harbour. In the 14th century it was eventually paved. Such is its significance today that the Barcelonans have coined two new words – *ramblejar*, to walk down the Rambla and *ramblista*, someone who loves to *ramblejar*.

Monument a Colom

This monumental column at the seaward end of the Ramblas is crowned by a statue of Christopher Columbus, pointing to the horizon with an outstretched arm. It commemorates the great navigator's return to Barcelona from his first voyage to the Americas in 1493. It was erected outside the naval headquarters of Catalonia during the 1888 Universal Exhibition and, from the top, it affords spectacular views of the seafront.

ⓐ Plaça del Portal de la Pau ⓣ 933 025 224 ⓛ 10.00–18.30 Oct–May, 09.00–20.30 June–Sept ⓜ Metro: Drassanes

Plaça del Rei

The delightful 'King's Square' was once a busy medieval marketplace. Today it is a fascinating ensemble of architectural styles. One side is occupied by the **Palau Reial Major** (Great Royal Palace) – the former residence of the Counts of Barcelona, constructed in the 11th century. It was on the steps leading up to

ⓞ *Human statue outside the Catedral*

the palace that King Ferdinand and Queen Isabella are believed to have received Columbus on his return from the Americas in 1493. On the north side of the square, the Gothic **Capella de Santa Agata** (Chapel of St Agatha) was constructed on the old Roman wall. Opposite, the **Palau de Lloctinent** (Palace of the Deputy) was built in 1549 for the Catalan representative of the king. There are marvellous views of the medieval city from the top of the five-storey **Mirador de Rei Martí** (Tower of King Martí). The **Museu d'Història de la Ciutat** (City History Museum, see page 65) is also in the square.

ⓐ Plaça del Rei Ⓜ Metro Jaume I

Plaça Reial

This charming porticoed square, flanked by bars and restaurants and adorned by palm trees and an ornamental fountain, was constructed in 1848. Some of the façades are decorated with sculpted terracotta reliefs of celebrated navigators and the two tree-like central lamp-posts were Gaudí's first commission in Barcelona. On Sunday mornings there is a coin and stamp market here.

ⓐ Plaça Reial Ⓜ Metro: Liceu

Plaça de Sant Jaume

This square is situated on the site of the former forum and marketplace of Roman *Barcino*. Today it represents the city's political hub. On its south side stands the impressive Catalan Gothic **Ajuntament** (Town Hall), seat of the city's government. The first floor contains the famous old council chamber, the Saló de Cent (Chamber of One Hundred), with its patriotic tapestries. Across the square, the Renaissance **Palau de la Generalitat**

(Government Palace) is home to the government of Catalonia.
③ Plaça de Sant Jaume ⓝ Metro: Jaume I

Plaça de Sant Josep Oriol

This lively, picturesque square is known as the 'Montmartre of Barcelona', where local artists display their works at weekends and buskers entertain the crowds relaxing on the café terraces.

The 14th-century church of Santa Maria del Pi (named after the pine trees that once grew here) is typical of the Catalan Gothic style,

◆ Buskers in Plaça de Sant Josep Oriol

with its solid exterior, predominantly horizontal lines and lack of sculptural ornament. The entrance to the church is in a small adjoining square, Plaça del Pi – once site of the parish cemetery, but today the venue of a farmers' market at weekends.
ⓐ Plaça de Sant Josep Oriol Ⓝ Metro: Liceu

Plaça de la Seu (Cathedral Square)

This spacious square is a popular meeting point and also draws a number of buskers and street entertainers. On Sundays, locals gather at noon to perform the *sardana*, a Catalan folk dance, before the Cathedral's ornate and imposing façade. Between the east side of the Cathedral and Via Laietana lie the remnants of the ancient Roman walls.
ⓐ Plaça de la Seu Ⓝ Metro: Liceu or Jaume I

CULTURE

Catedral

Barcelona's mighty Gothic Cathedral was constructed on the remains of a palaeo-Christian basilica and a Romanesque church. Dedicated to St Eulàlia, who was martyred by the Romans in the 4th century for her Christian beliefs, it is considered one of the finest examples of Catalan Gothic architecture.

The majestic interior is a harmonious fusion of medieval and Renaissance style, and the Chapel of Christ of Lepanto is its finest example of Gothic architecture. Don't miss the tranquil 14th-century cloister, with its shaded gardens, pond and even a small gaggle of white geese, said to symbolise the virginal purity of St Eulàlia.
ⓐ Plaça de la Seu ⓣ 933 151 554 ⓛ 08.00–13.15, 16.30–19.30 Ⓝ Metro: Liceu or Jaume I

Gran Teatre del Liceu

For over 150 years, the Liceu has been Spain's foremost opera house, hosting world-class performers ever since its inauguration in 1847. However, it has an extremely chequered history: it was tragically burned down in 1861, and rebuilt only to be bombed in 1893. It was restored to its former glory, then went up in flames again in 1994. Once more it rose from the ashes in 1999, but this time with improved acoustics, a larger stage and state-of-the-art machinery. Guided tours of the interior provide a unique insight into the workings of the theatre.

ⓐ La Rambla 51–59 ⓣ 934 859 914 ⓦ www.liceubarcelona.com ⓔ visites@liceubarcelona.com ⓛ guided tours at 10.00 (one hour); 'express' tours at 11.30, 12.00 and 13.00 (15–20 minutes) ⓜ Metro: Liceu

Museu d'Història de la Ciutat (City History Museum)

This fascinating museum recounts the city's evolution through 2,000 years of history, in a series of locations around the **Plaça del Rei** (see page 60). Start at the impressive underground walkways beneath the square, which reveal the ancient foundations of the Roman settlement of *Barcino*.

The main section of the museum is housed in a medieval mansion, and vividly traces the story of Barcelona from a simple Roman trading-post to a wealthy 18th-century metropolis. The museum ticket also includes entry to the **Saló del Tinell**, the spacious barrel-vaulted banqueting hall of the **Palau Reial Major** (see page 60); the royal chapel, the **Capella de Santa Agata** (see page 62); and the **Mirador del Rei Martí** (see page 62).

ⓐ Plaça del Rei, Carrer del Veguer 2 ⓣ 933 151 111 ⓦ www.museuhistoria.bcn.es ⓔ museuhistoria@mail.bcn.es ⓛ 10.00–20.00 Tues–Sat, 10.00–15.00 Sun, June–Sept; 10.00–14.00,

16.00–20.00 Tues–Sat, 10.00–15.00 Sun, Oct–May. Also night visits: 21.00–23.30 Mon–Tues, July; 21.00–23.30 Tues–Wed, Aug–Sept
Ⓜ Metro: Jaume I

Museu Frederic Marès (Frederic Marès Museum)

This eccentric museum, at the heart of the Gothic Quarter, was founded and donated to the city by sculptor Frederic Marès i Deulovol (1893–1991). It comprises two sections: the sculpture collection, with artefacts from pre-Roman times through to the 20th century; and the 'Sentimental Museum', portraying daily life from the 15th to the 20th centuries through an extraordinary array of curios and household objects. Entrance to the museum is via a beautiful medieval courtyard garden, once part of the Royal Palace of the Kings and Queens of Catalonia and Aragon.
Ⓐ Plaça Sant Iu 5–6 Ⓣ 933 105 800 Ⓦ www.museumares.bcn.es
Ⓔ museumares@mail.bcn.es Ⓛ 10.00–19.00 Tues–Sat, 10.00–15.00 Sun Ⓜ Metro: Jaume I

RETAIL THERAPY

There are plenty of shops to choose from here, from the fashion boutiques of stylish Avinguda del Portal de l'Angel, a busy pedestrian thoroughfare, to the more old-fashioned specialist stores of the Barri Gotic. Here too, La Boqueria market (see page 68) is the best of over 40 food markets in town, and a must-see, even if you're not hungry!

Antiques, books & music

Angel Batlle This antiquarian bookshop contains a fascinating collection of old maps, prints and nautical charts.
Ⓐ Carrer Palla 23 Ⓣ 301 58 84 Ⓜ Metro: Liceu

L'Arca de l'Avia A treasure trove of antique cottons, linens and silks.
🅐 Carrer Banys Nous 20 🅣 933 021 598 🅜 Metro: Liceu
Artur Ramon Anticuario Browse among the paintings, furniture and
valuable *objets d'art* in Barcelona's best antique store. 🅐 Carrer de la
Palla 25 🅣 933 025 970 🅜 Metro: Jaume I
Casa Beethoven Specialist music shop with an impressive stock of
scores and sheet music, especially by Spanish and Catalan
composers. 🅐 La Rambla 97 🅣 933 014 826 🅜 Metro: Liceu
Jordi Capell This specialist bookshop, housed in the basement of the
College of Architects, focuses on architecture and design. 🅐 Plaça
Nova 5 🅣 934 123 788 🅜 Metro: Jaume I

Arts & crafts

Sala Parés Barcelona's top gallery specialing in 19th- and 20th-century
artworks. 🅐 Carrer Petritxol 5 🅣 933 187 020 🅜 Metro: Catalunya
Germanes Garcia A country-style shop selling wickerwork of all shapes
and sizes. 🅐 Carrer Banys Nous 15 🅣 933 186 646 🅜 Metro: Liceu

🔴 *Weighing things up at the Mercat de la Boqueria*

La Manual Alpargatera An old-fashioned shop producing all manner of straw-woven items, including handmade traditional Spanish espadrilles with esparto soles. Carrer Avinýo 7 933 010 172 Metro: Jaume I

Fashion
MNG Cheap, trendy designs for young fashionistas. Carrer Portal de l'Angel 933 176 985 www.mango.com Metro Catalunya

Food
Mercat de la Boqueria Barcelona's main covered market is a veritable showcase of Catalan gastronomic delights, from fruit, herbs and vegetables to meat, fish and crustaceans. The cavernous market hall is best entered through an impressive wrought-iron gateway off La Rambla. Inside is a riot of noise and activity, as market sellers, local shoppers, restaurateurs and tourists all jostle for the best buys of the day, and to taste the specialities of the region. It is an excellent place to stock up for a picnic or simply to soak up the flavours, colours and fragrances of the Mediterranean. La Rambla 100 933 182 017 07.00–20.00 Mon–Sat, closed Sun Metro: Liceu

Miscellaneous
Cereria Subira The city's oldest shop, founded in 1761, sells a staggering variety of candles, both religious and profane. Baixada Llibreteria 7 933 152 606 Metro: Jaume I

El Ingenio Come to this old-fashioned magic shop for tricks, games and carnival masks. Carrer Rauric 6–8 933 177 138 Metro: Jaume I

TAKING A BREAK

Ambos Mundos £ ① Soak up the atmosphere on the terrace of this popular *cerveceria* (beer bar) in atmospheric Plaça Reial. ⓐ Plaça Reial 9–10 ☎ 933 170 166 🕐 Closed Tues Ⓜ Metro: Liceu

Bar del Pi £ ② This pint-sized bar serves delicious coffee and a small selection of tapas al fresco. ⓐ Plaça Sant Josep Oriol 1 ☎ 933 022 123 Ⓜ Metro: Liceu

Dulcinea £ ③ The most famous chocolate shop in town and the place to try *suizos* (hot chocolate) served with *melindros* (sugar-topped sponge-fingers) for dunking. The milkshakes and cakes are scrumptious too. ⓐ Carrer de Petrixol 2 ☎ 933 026 842 Ⓜ Metro: Liceu

Mesón del Café £ ④ A tiny locals' café, serving excellent coffee and hot chocolate. ⓐ Carrer de la Libreteria 16 ☎ 933 150 754 🕐 Closed Sun Ⓜ Metro: Liceu

AFTER DARK

Restaurants
Avoid the over-priced restaurants along La Rambla and head into the narrow alleys and atmospheric squares of the Barri Gòtic for some of the best eateries in town.

Can Culleretes £ ⑤ Enjoy robust country-style Catalan cuisine in an atmospheric, rustic setting in one of the city's oldest restaurants. Game is a speciality in season. ⓐ Carrer d'en Quintana 5 ☎ 933 176 485 🕐 Closed Sun evening & Mon Ⓜ Metro: Liceu

Egipto £ ❼ This small popular restaurant by La Boqueria market serves hearty Catalan cuisine made with fresh market produce. ⓐ La Rambla 79 ❶ 933 179 545 Ⓝ Metro: Liceu

Els Quatre Gats £ ❼ Local artists and writers popularised this beautiful *Modernista* café in the early 1900s. Even the menu was designed by Picasso. Today it serves simple Catalan staples. ⓐ Carrer de Montsió 3 ❶ 933 024 140 ❶ 09.00–00.30 Ⓝ Metro: Catalunya

La Fonda £–££ ❽ A buzzy designer restaurant, serving a good variety of stylish yet affordable Mediterranean dishes. ⓐ Passatge Escudellers 1 ❶ 933 017 515 Ⓝ Metro: Liceu

Les Quinze Nits £–££ ❾ One of the Ciutat Vella's most popular restaurants. Ask for a table on the terrace overlooking the square, and tuck into a delicious seafood platter, paella or rabbit stew. Be prepared to queue. ⓐ Plaça Reial 5 ❶ 933 173 075 Ⓝ Metro: Liceu

Pitarra ££ ❿ This old-fashioned restaurant, named after the 19th-century Catalan playwright who once lived here, is known for its delicious paella. ⓐ Carrer d'Avinyó 56 ❶ 933 011 647 ❶ Closed Sun Ⓝ Metro: Liceu

Taxidermista ££ ⓫ A lively restaurant, in an old taxidermist's studio, offering modern Mediterranean cuisine amid original cast-iron pillars and black-and-white marble floors. ⓐ Plaça Reial 8 ❶ 934 124 536 Ⓝ Metro: Liceu

Agut d'Avignon £££ 🔟 This illustrious Catalan restaurant counts the King of Spain among its patrons. It's best to make a reservation if you want to be one. ⓐ Carrer de la Trinitat 3/Carrer d'Avinyó 8 ❶ 933 026 034 ❶ 12.00–24.00 Ⓝ Metro: Jaume I or Liceu

Bars & clubs

Café del Òpera The best café-bar on La Rambla – atmospheric, intimate and still with its original 19th-century décor. ⓐ La Rambla 74 ❶ 93 302 41 80 Ⓝ Metro: Liceu

Hard Rock Café Part of the world-famous chain and a popular meeting place for the young crowd. ⓐ Plaça de Catalunya 21 ❶ 93 270 23 05 Ⓦ www.hardrock.com Ⓝ Metro: Catalunya

Harlem Jazz Club Small, atmospheric, and a choice nightspot for live jazz and blues. ⓐ Carrer Comtessa de Sobradiel 8 ❶ 93 310 07 55 ❶ 20.00–04.00 Tues–Sun, closed Mon Ⓝ Metro: Jaume I

Jamboree A hugely popular venue for live blues, jazz, soul, funk and occasional hip-hop until midnight when it becomes a funky dance club. The adjoining **Tarantos** bar develops from flamenco joint to lively salsa club as the night progresses. ⓐ Plaça Reial 17 ❶ 933 191 789 Ⓦ www.masimas.com/jamboree ❶ 22.00–late Ⓝ Metro: Liceu

CULTURE

Gran Teatre del Liceu Barcelona's celebrated belle époque opera house (see page 64). ⓐ La Rambla 51–9 ❶ 934 859 900 Ⓦ www.liceubarcelona.com Ⓝ Metro: Liceu

La Barceloneta & La Ribera

With so much to see and do in the old town, it is easy to forget that Barcelona is a seaside city, with its fine sandy beaches, marinas and a giant waterfront leisure complex, Maremagnum. La Ribera (The Waterfront) was the medieval city's thriving maritime and trading district. In the 10th century, a settlement grew up here along what was then the seashore. Nowadays, it is a smart, in-vogue *barri* (quarter), brimming with trendy boutiques and sophisticated bars and restaurants.

The atmospheric neighbouring district of La Barceloneta was constructed on a triangular wedge of reclaimed land in the mid-18th century. With its narrow streets and ramshackle houses, over the centuries it has retained all the charm of an old Mediterranean fishing village, and boasts some of the finest seafood restaurants in town.

SIGHTS & ATTRACTIONS

L'Aquàrium de Barcelona (Barcelona Aquarium)

Barcelona's ultra-modern Aquarium is one of the finest in Europe, with over 10,000 exotic sea creatures. The main highlight is an 80 m (260 ft) glass tunnel, called the Oceanarium, which plunges you straight into the midst of sharks, sting rays, moonfish and other multi-coloured species.

🄰 Moll d'Espanya 🄰 932 217 474 🄰 10.00–14.00, 16.00–20.00 Mon–Sat 🄰 Metro: Drassanes or Barceloneta

Beaches

Barcelona's beaches offer bathers and sun-worshippers some of the cleanest city sea-bathing in the Mediterranean, with nearly

La Barceloneta & La Ribera

0   250 metres
0   250 yards

Metro Stop Ⓜ
Cathedral ✝
Information ⓘ
Police Station ✕
Airport ✈
Railway Stn 🚂
Bus Station 🚌
Hospital ✚

N

5 km (3 miles) of clean, broad, sandy beaches stretching from La Barceloneta northwards. Facilities include playgrounds, good disabled access, lifeguards, showers, bars, shops and restaurants. The three beaches nearest the city – Platjes Sant Miquel, Sant Sebastià and Barceloneta – get very crowded on hot days, so it is worth heading farther north, off Avinguda del Litoral, to Platjes Nova Icària, Bogatell, Mar Bella (a nudist beach) or Nova Mar Bella, where there are windsurfers and small craft for hire during summer months.

The beaches are fringed by the Passeig Marítim – the palm-lined boardwalk linking La Barceloneta to La Vila Olímpica, Hotel Arts and Frank Gehry's glittering copper *Fish* sculpture – the city's new maritime symbol.

Ⓝ Metro: Barceloneta, Ciutadella or Bogatell

La Barceloneta

The quaint old district of La Barceloneta (Little Barcelona) was traditionally the home of seamen and port workers, and the clock-tower on the Moll de la Barceloneta was once a lighthouse. There is still an air of nostalgia in the traditional-style cafés, along the quayside lined with brightly painted fishing boats and nets, and in the criss-cross grid of ancient narrow streets, where children play football while locals sit and chat, their colourful washing fluttering overhead on the wrought-iron balconies. The heart of the district is the **Plaça de la Barceloneta**, with the beautiful baroque church of Sant Miquel del Port (Barceloneta's patron saint) and splashing fountains, where locals still come to collect drinking water.

Ⓝ Metro: Barceloneta

Las Golondrinas

The best way to see the old harbour and port area is to climb aboard one of the tour boats called *golondrinas* (swallows). Harbour tours depart regularly in summer and once an hour on winter weekends; excursions to the Port Olímpic operate several times a day during summer.

ⓐ Porta de la Pau ⓘ 934 423 106 ⓦ www.lasgolondrinas.com
Ⓜ Metro: Drassanes

🔺 *Stroll along the quayside in La Barceloneta*

El Born (The Born)

The tiny 'Born' district has recently emerged as one of the trendier quarters of town, buzzing by day with funky shops, galleries and craft workshops; and with fashionable bars and restaurants by night. Its main thoroughfare is the **Passeig del Born**. The name of this avenue means 'to joust' and for many centuries from the Middle Ages onwards, it was the scene of many city festivals, processions, tournaments, fairs, markets and carnivals. During the Inquisition, heretics were burned here. Today it plays host to a number of popular cafés and restaurants.

One end of the Passeig is dominated by the imposing church of Santa Maria del Mar (see page 78). At the other end, the old **Mercat del Born** (Born Market) – a glass and wrought-iron structure from the 1870s – is a magnificent example of 19th-century industrial architecture. Until 1971, it housed the city's main wholesale food market. Then, in 2001, some of the most extensive medieval archaeological remains in Europe were discovered here. The building is currently being converted into a major new cultural centre.

Ⓝ Metro: Barceloneta or Jaume I

Parc de la Ciutadella (Citadel Park)

This large leafy park is the green lung of Barcelona. It takes its name from the mighty citadel which dominated the city in the 18th century. In its midst are a boating lake, playgrounds, lawns, promenades, the Parc Zoològic (see page 77) and a showy fountain – the Font Monumental – which Gaudí contributed to as a student. Notable buildings include the arsenal of the former citadel and the Castell dels Tres Dragons (Three Dragons Castle), a striking *Modernista* building which contains the Museu de Ciènces Naturals (Museum of Natural Science).

ⓐ Museu de Ciènces Naturals: Parc de la Ciutadella ☎ 933 196 912

Ⓦ www.bcn.es/museuciences Ⓔ museuciences@mail.bcn.es
Ⓛ 10.00–14.30 Tues, Wed, Fri–Sun, 10.00–18.30 Thur Ⓝ Metro:
Barceloneta

Parc Zoològic (Zoo)

Spain's leading zoo, with over 7,500 animals of 400 different species
from all over the world, is always a popular outing with children,
especially the under-fives who love the petting farm, the mini-train
and the splashy shows of the dolphinarium.
Ⓐ Parc de la Ciutadella Ⓣ 932 256 780 Ⓦ www.zoobarcelona.com
Ⓛ 10.00–17.00 (until 18.00 Mar–May, Oct; until 19.00 June–Sept)
Ⓝ Metro: Ciutadella

Port Vell (Old Port)

No other single Olympic project changed the face of the city as
dramatically as the construction of Port Vell. This former industrial
area of ships and sprawling warehouses has undergone massive
transformation and is now a popular recreation area, with an
aquarium, a cinema complex and Maremagnum
(www.maremagnum.es), a huge shopping centre with cafés, bars and
restaurants. Approach it via the Rambla de Mar, a series of undulating
wooden walkways and wavelike metal arches, which stretches out
over the sea like a watery extension of La Rambla (see page 58).
Ⓝ Metro: Drassanes

Port Olímpic (Olympic Harbour)

Another enduring mark of the 1992 Olympics is the Olympic Harbour –
now a popular Mediterranean mooring for passing yachtspeople, with
lively quaysides lined with cafés, bars, restaurants and nightclubs.
Ⓝ Metro: Ciutadella

Santa Maria del Mar (Saint Mary of the Sea)

The magnificent Gothic Basilica of Santa Maria del Mar is arguably
Barcelona's finest church, striking in its simplicity. It lies at the heart
of La Ribera. The original settlement grew up around a tiny 10th-
century chapel here called Santa Maria de les Arenes (Saint Mary of
the Sands), built on what was then the seashore. During the 14th
century, it was transformed into today's imposing 'seaside cathedral'
as a show of the city's maritime power. The foundation stone
commemorates the Catalan conquest of Sardinia.

⬤ *Street sculpture – Gambrinus by Xavier Mariscal*

The bland façade belies a majestic spacious interior of slim octagonal columns and narrow lofty naves. The church is surprisingly lacking in ornamentation, as most of its treasures were lost during the Spanish Civil War. However, the 15th-century ship atop the altar serves as a reminder of the city's seafaring heyday.

🄰 Passeig del Born 1 🄣 933 102 390 🄛 09.00–13.30, 16.30–20.00
🄝 Metro: Barceloneta

Vila Olímpica (Olympic Village)

The formerly run-down area of Poble Nou, just behind the Port Olímpic, was developed into the Olympic Village, the residential area for 15,000 competitors. After the Games, this high-tech corridor of apartment blocks, shops and offices became a popular place for Barcelonans to live, work and relax.

🄝 Metro: Ciutadella

CULTURE

Museu d'Història de Catalunya (History Museum of Catalonia)

The Palau de Mar (Palace of the Sea), the port's old general warehouse, is a fine example of 19th-century industrial architecture. Nowadays, it contains the History Museum of Catalonia, a fascinating hands-on museum illustrating the great moments of the region's history and providing a valuable insight into Catalan lifestyle over the centuries. The museum café, on the top floor of the Palau de Mar, offers one of the best views of the city.

🄰 Palau de Mar, Plaça Pau Vila 3 🄣 932 254 700 🄦 www.mhcat.net
🄔 mhc.cultura@gencat.net 🄛 10.00–20.00 Tues, 10.00–19.00
Wed–Sat, 10.00–14.30 Sun 🄝 Metro: Barceloneta

Museu Picasso

Not only is this museum the city's greatest tourist attraction, but it is also the most important and most complete collection of artworks by Pablo Picasso in the world. Although the great Spanish artist was born in Andalucia, he moved to Barcelona in 1895, when he was just 14 years old, and spent some of his most formative years here.

The outstanding collection is housed in three adjoining medieval mansions on the beautiful Carrer Montcada. It traces Picasso's career from early childhood sketches and impressionistic landscapes to the more mature, distinctive works of later years, and demonstrates his versatility and extraordinary artistic development over the decades.

ⓐ Carrer Montcada 15–23 ⓣ 933 196 310
ⓦ www.museupicasso.bcn.es ⓔ museupicasso@mail.bcn.es
ⓛ 10.00–20.00 Tues–Sun ⓜ Metro: Jaume I

Museu Tèxtil i de la Indumentària (Textile and Clothing Museum)

This delightful museum is housed in a beautiful 14th-century palace on one of Barcelona's most aristocratic streets. It illustrates how the city rose to prosperity during the 1800s, thanks to its thriving textile industry, with sumptuous displays of tapestries, textiles, lace, clothing and accessories dating from medieval to modern times.

ⓘ Carrer Montcada 12–14 ⓣ 933 104 516 ⓦ www.museutextil.bcn.es
ⓔ museutextil@mailbcn.es ⓛ 10.00–18.00 Tues–Sat, 10.00–15.00 Sun ⓜ Metro: Jaume I

Palau de la Música Catalana (Palace of Catalan Music)

This dazzling palace, built in the pure *Modernista* style by Domenech i Montaner in 1908, is considered one of the finest concert houses in the world. Each year it hosts some 300 concerts, with an attendance of over half a million people. In a city full of architectural wonders, it stands out as one of the greatest works of Modernism and a symbol of the renaissance of Catalan culture. Indeed, in 1997 it was declared a World Heritage Site by UNESCO. If you have time, go to a concert – it's much the best way to enjoy the building.

🅐 Carrer de Sant Francesc de Paula 2 📞 932 681 000 🕐 10.00–15.30
Ⓜ Metro: Urquinaona

RETAIL THERAPY

Art & design
Galeria Maeght A prestigious gallery of 20th-century art, design and photography. 🅐 Carrer Montcada 25 (1st floor) 📞 933 014 245
Ⓜ Metro: Jaume I

Ici et La Small but innovative design shop, brimming with fun furniture and home accessories by young Spanish designers.
🅐 Carrer Espaseria 2 📞 933 102 309 Ⓜ Metro: Barceloneta

Museu Picasso An excellent museum shop, brimming with Picasso-inspired souvenirs and gifts. 🅐 Carrer Montcada 15 📞 933 196 310
Ⓜ Metro: Jaume I

Fashion & accessories
Alea Tiny boutique at the heart of La Ribera, showcasing up-and-coming Catalan jewellers. 🅐 Carrer Argenteria 66 📞 933 101 373
Ⓜ Metro: Jaume I or Barceloneta

Maremagnum A huge waterfront leisure complex with numerous fashion boutiques including Calvin Klein, Lacoste, Quiksilver, Woman's Secret and top local designer, Adolfo Dominguez.

🅐 Maremagnum, Moll d'Espanya 🕾 932 258 100

🅦 www.maremagnum.es Ⓜ Metro: Barceloneta or Drassanes

TAKING A BREAK

Can Ramonet £ ❶ Tuck into some tasty seafood at this stand-up tapas bar attached to Barceloneta's top-notch fish restaurant.

🔘 *Frank Gehry's* Fish *sculpture outside the Hotel Arts on the seafront*

Ⓐ Carrer Maquinista 17 Ⓣ 933 193 064 Ⓛ Closed Sun evening
Ⓝ Metro: Barceloneta

Hivernacle £ ❷ An elegant café, inside Ciutadella park's beautiful
19th-century greenhouse, sometimes with live jazz or classical
music. Ⓐ Passeig de Picasso Ⓣ 934 132 400 Ⓝ Metro: Arc de Triomf

Tèxtil Cafè £ ❸ No need to pay the museum entry to enjoy this café
in a beautiful courtyard adjoining the Museu Tèxtil (see page 80).
Ⓐ Carrer Montcada 12 Ⓣ 932 682 598 Ⓝ Metro: Jaume I

AFTER DARK

Restaurants

Most people head to La Barceloneta to eat in its smart harbourside seafood restaurants – a prime location for paella and people-watching – while La Ribera boasts a handful of fashionable bistros and brasseries.

Cal Pep £ ❹ A tiny simple locals' restaurant specialising in seafood. Sit at the bar and try some of the mouth-watering tapas. ⓐ Plaça de les Olles 8 ❶ 933 107 961 ◐ Closed Mon lunch & Sun Ⓜ Metro: Barceloneta or Jaume I

El Cangrejo Loco ££ ❺ Superb fish restaurant in the Olympic Port. Try the *fideua* (seafood paella) or a seafood platter. ⓐ Moll de Gregal 29–30 ❶ 932 210 533 Ⓦ www.elcangrejoloco.com Ⓜ Metro: Ciutadella

L'Ou com Balla ££ ❻ Fusion cuisine in a romantic candlelit venue in La Ribera. ⓐ Carrer Banys Vells 20 ❶ 933 105 378 ◐ Evenings only Ⓜ Metro: Jaume I

ABAC £££ ❼ Michelin-starred chef, Xavier Pellicier, serves exceptional Spanish haute cuisine in this elegant minimalist restaurant. ⓐ Carrer Rec 79–89 ❶ 933 196 600 Ⓦ www.restaurantabac.com ◐ Closed Mon lunch & Sun Ⓜ Metro: Barceloneta

Can Majó £££ ❽ Barcelona's top seafood restaurant. ⓐ Carrer Almirall Aixada 23 ❶ 932 215 455 ◐ 10.00–24.00 Ⓜ Metro: Barceloneta

Hofmann £££ ❾ Eponymous restaurant of Mey Hofmann, one
of Spain's top chefs. ⓐ Carrer Argenteria 74–8 ❶ 933 195 889
ⓦ www.hofmann-bcn.com ❶ Closed Sat & Sun ⓝ Metro: Jaume I

Set Portes £££ ❿ A veritable Barcelona institution, with waiters
in long white aprons serving fine Catalan cuisine in a traditional
setting. ⓐ Passeig de Isabel II 14 ❶ 933 193 033
ⓦ www.setportes.com ❶ 13.00–01.00 ⓝ Metro: Barceloneta

Bars & clubs
Baja Beach Club A lively discotheque on a Californian beach theme,
with a wide variety of music to suit all tastes. ⓐ Passeig Marítim 34
(local 3) ❶ 933 218 573

Le Kashba An intimate Moroccan-style bar playing easy listening,
minimal, house, funk, latin and jazz sounds. ⓐ Plaça Pau Vila

Razzmatazz Five different dance floors under one roof, each
with different music genres and some of the city's top DJs.
ⓐ Carrer Almogavers 122 ⓦ www.salarazzmatazz.com
ⓝ Metro: Marina

El Xampanyet A tiny champagne bar with blue-tiled walls, marble
tables and zinc bar, combining old-fashioned charm with a lively,
young crowd. ⓐ Carrer Montcada 22 ❶ 933 197 003

Live music
La Cova del Drac One of the city's top jazz venues, featuring
international names and local talent. ⓐ Carrer Vallmajor 33 ❶ 933
191 798 ⓦ www.masimas.com ⓝ Metro: Muntaner

Cinema

Cinesa Maremagnum A large modern eight-screen cinema complex beside the sea, showing a variety of Spanish- and English-language films. ❷ Port Vell ❶ 932 333 231 Ⓜ Metro: Drassanes

IMAX Port Vell Think big with this giant wrap-around 3-D screen. ❸ Carrer Moll d'Espanya ❶ 932 351 111 Ⓦ www.imaxportvell.com ❹ Metro: Drassanes

Culture

This area contains two of the city's main concert venues. There are also occasional concerts and recitals in the Basilica of Santa Maria del Mar (see page 78), and open-air theatre, concerts and dance events in Parc de la Ciutadella (see page 76) during summer.

L'Auditori This modern arts complex is home to the National Catalan Orchestra. The Sala Simfònica stages full orchestral concerts while the more intimate Sala Polivante is popular for recitals and chamber ensembles. After night performances, the Arts Bus runs concert-goers to Plaça de Catalunya. ❸ Carrer Lepant 150 ❶ 932 479 300 Ⓦ www.auditori.org Ⓜ Metro: Marina

Palau de la Música Catalana Undoubtedly the most spectacular venue for classical music in town, staging frequent concerts by the Cor de Cambra (Chamber Choir) del Palau de la Música, or by the amateur Orfeó Català choir, for whom the auditorium was originally built (see page 80). ❷ Carrer Sant Francesc de Paula 2 ❶ 932 681 000 Ⓜ Metro: Urquinaona

● *Enjoy a leisurely lunch in La Barceloneta*

86

L'Eixample & Gràcia

L'Eixample (The Extension) was built between 1860 and 1920 to accommodate the burgeoning bourgeois population, and to merge the outlying villages of Sants, Sarrià-Sant Gervasi and Gràcia into the modern city. Its construction coincided with the emergence of Catalan *Modernisme*, and many of its wealthy new residents commissioned the great architects of the day to design grand mansions for them in this flamboyant new style. As a consequence, the district resembles a huge open-air museum, containing most of the city's greatest *Modernista* landmarks, including Gaudí's legendary Sagrada Família church, Parc Güell and La Pedrera. Today the Eixample remains a wealthy district, brimming with designer boutiques, smart hotels, sophisticated bars and restaurants.

To the north, the 'village' of Gràcia has long been known as a radical centre of Catalanism and, despite being completely engulfed by the city these days, the district still maintains a village atmosphere and the locals consider themselves Graciencs rather than Barcelonans.

CERDÀ'S EIXAMPLE

Ildefons Cerdà's geometric grid design for the Eixample was an innovative plan in its day, which broke completely with former models of Spanish urban planning. It divided the city into 550 symmetrical blocks covering an area of 23 sq km (9 sq miles), with the aptly named Avinguda Diagonal cutting through the blocks at a 45° angle to add a touch of quirkiness.

SIGHTS & ATTRACTIONS

Casa Amatller (Amatller House)

Casa Amatller was designed for local chocolate manufacturer
Antonio Amatller i Costa by one of the great exponents of Catalan
Modernisme, Puig i Cadafalch, in 1900. With its stepped gable and
neo-Gothic façade adorned by sculptures, coats of arms and
wrought-iron work, it is one of the most impressive houses on the
Passeig de Gràcia (see page 97). The beautifully crafted wooden lift
within the broad entranceway was one of Barcelona's earliest
elevators, and one interior doorway has some charming carvings
showing animals making chocolate!

   The building currently houses the **Centre del Modernisme**, which
provides information and multilingual guides on the *Ruta del
Modernisme* (see page 153).

ⓐ Passeig de Gràcia 41 ❶ 934 880 139 Ⓜ Metro: Passeig de Gràcia

Casa Batlló (Batlló House)

The flamboyant Casa Batlló stands in stark contrast to its neighbour,
Casa Amatller. Designed by Gaudí in 1907, with a dazzling multi-
coloured façade and sensuous wavelike iron and stone curves,
it is one of the most famous buildings of the *Modernista* school.
The design is said to represent the triumph of St George over the
dragon (see page 13). An audio-guided tour of the extraordinary
interior, and the rooftop with its unique chimneys, reveals
Gaudí's unparalleled freedom of imagination and abstract
genius.

ⓐ Passeig de Gràcia 43 ❶ 932 160 306 Ⓦ www.casabatllo.es
ⓔ infovisites@casabatllo.es ⓛ 09.00–20.00 Ⓜ Metro: Passeig
de Gràcia

🔺 Modernista *architecture in L'Eixample*

Casa Lleó-Morera (Lleó-Morera House)

This decorative *Modernista* mansion is considered architect Lluís Domènech i Montaner's most beautiful and exuberant work. Built between 1902 and 1906, it is characterised by its striking neo-Gothic façade, which minimises the corner by placing visual emphasis on decorative circular balconies, columned galleries and oriel windows.

🔵 Passeig de Gràcia 35 Ⓜ Metro: Passeig de Gràcia

MANZANA DE LA DISCORDIA

The most impressive block on the Passeig de Gràcia (between Carrer d'Aragó and Carrer Consell de Cent) is called the Manzana de la Discordia (Block of Discord), because of the clashing architectural styles of Casa Amatller, Casa Batlló and Casa Lleó-Morera (see pages 90–1) – three of the most celebrated architectural ensembles and a magnificent showcase for the city's greatest exponents of *Modernisme*, Montaner, Cadafalch and Gaudí. View them by day and by night, when their façades are magically lit.

Casa Milà – 'La Pedrera' (Milà House – 'The Stone Quarry')

Gaudí was at the peak of his architectural career when he constructed the extraordinary apartment block of Casa Milà for dilettante politician, Pere Milà in 1912. It was Gaudí's last and most famous secular building, and also one of his most inventive – a triumph of aesthetics over practicality, built entirely on columns and arches, with sinuous lines and rippling limestone façades, supposedly without a single straight line or right-angled corner. Every last detail of design was carried out by the great Catalan architect, right down to the crooked banisters, stylish doorknobs, balconies of recycled wrought-ironwork, and glass-encrusted chimneys of the roof terrace.

Sadly, soon after its construction, Casa Milà was to become Spain's most controversial apartment block. Its innovative appearance so shocked Barcelonans when it was built that they nicknamed it 'La Pedrera' ('The Stone Quarry'). After years of neglect, it was posthumously declared a World Heritage Site by UNESCO in

1984 (the first 20th-century building to achieve the honour) and, ironically, it is now one of the city's most admired buildings.

Inside the building is the fascinating Espai Gaudí, an exhibition about the origins and construction of Casa Milà, with drawings, models, photographs and audiovisuals. But the highlight of any visit is undoubtedly the extraordinary undulating roof with its strangely shaped chimney-stacks and amazing bird's-eye vistas of the Eixample. During summer weekends, the roof terrace is the

◯ Rooftop chimneys at Casa Milà 'La Pedrera'

spectacular venue for *La Pedrera de Nit*, a series of open-air evening concerts.

🅐 Passeig de Gràcia 92 ☎ 934 845 995 🕓 10.00–20.00 Ⓜ Metro: Diagonal

Hospital de la Santa Creu i de San Pau

This beautiful unusual hospital complex forms one of Europe's finest ensembles of Modernism, designed by the innovative architect Domènech i Montaner. Not only did he defy the orderliness of the Eixample by aligning the buildings at 45° to the street grid, but he also broke with the tradition of having one large hospital building, by creating a 'hospital-village' of 48 small pavilions, connected by a series of underground passages. Construction began in 1902 and, when the hospital was eventually inaugurated in 1930, it was considered among the most advanced in Europe. Sadly, today its future as a hospital is uncertain, due to the demands of modern-day medicine. However the entire complex is protected as a UNESCO World Heritage Site.

🅐 Carrer de Sant Antoni Maria Claret 167 Ⓜ Metro: Hospital de Sant Pau

Temple Expiatori de la Sagrada Família (Expiatory Temple of the Holy Family)

This extraordinary building is surely the most unusual cathedral in the world, and Barcelona's most distinctive landmark. It also represents the synthesis of architectural genius Antoni Gaudí's work. The first stone was laid in 1882 and the devout Catholic worked on the project for over 40 years. Such was his commitment to the building, he even lived in a workshop studio in the church for the last 15 years of his life. His dream was to create Europe's biggest cathedral and a bible in stone, with three façades representing the birth, death and resurrection of Christ, and 18 mosaic-clad domes and pinnacles to symbolise the 12 Apostles, the four Evangelists, the Virgin Mary and Christ.

Following his untimely death in 1926 (see page 13), only the crypt, the majority of the Nativity façade, the apse and just four towers were complete, but he left an overall plan of the project and numerous drawings which has enabled building work to continue.

◯ *Tip-top detail at La Sagrada Familia*

After his death, there was great controversy as to whether or not the work should resume. Since 1952 the Passion façade has been added and there are now eight completed towers, each over 100 m (325 ft) tall. There is a museum in the crypt, documenting the past, present and future of Gaudí's monumental, unfinished cathedral through photographs, plans, audiovisuals and original sketches, together with decorative items and maquettes of his life's work in general.

The entrance ticket includes admission to the building work in progress, the museum and access to the multi-coloured towers, either on foot or by lift, for breathtaking views of the city. The Nativity façade – devoted to the birth and early life of Christ with three doors representing Faith, Hope and Charity – is best viewed from the small park in Plaça Gaudí. The detail of sculpture on the façade is truly extraordinary, depicting almost 100 species of plants and as many types of animals, including Gaudí's beloved chameleons, which can be seen carved into the stonework all over the cathedral. By contrast, the post-Gaudi Passion façade, completed in 1990 by sculptor Josep Maria Subirachs, is more angular, minimalist and contemporary, signifying the pain and sacrifice of the final part of Christ's life. The main façade of the basilica, devoted to the Celestial Glory, has not yet been built.

It is estimated that there are a further 80 years of work, including the destruction of several buildings in surrounding streets, so it seems unlikely that Gaudí's great vision will ever be realised. Nevertheless, the Sagrada Família remains one of the great architectural wonders of the world and a must-see for every visitor to the city.

ⓐ Plaça de la Sagrada Família (church); Carrer Mallorca 401 (museum) ❶ 932 073 031 ⓦ www.sagradafamilia.org

ⓔ informa@sagradafamilia.org ⓛ 09.00–18.00 Oct–Feb; 09.00–20.00 Apr–Sept ⓝ Metro: Sagrada Família

Passeig de Gràcia

This broad leafy boulevard forms the axis of Cerdà's plan for the Eixample (see feature box on page 88) and is considered to be the 'Champs-Élysées of Catalonia'. It was constructed in 1827 on the same path as the original road which once joined Barcelona to the village of Gràcia, and today its central tree-lined pedestrian walkway forms a northern extension of La Rambla (see page 58). By the turn of the 20th century, it was one of the most sought-after residential streets, flanked by some of the city's most elegant and striking mansions. Other special features include the unusual Gaudíesque 'bench and lamp-post' ensembles. It was not until the 1920s that the boulevard became a major shopping thoroughfare. Still, today, it remains the hub of the city's shopping scene.

ⓐ Passeig de Gràcia ⓝ Metro: Passeig de Gràcia

Parc Güell

The wealthy Güell family commissioned a number of works from Antoni Gaudí over the years, including Palau Güell (see page 107) and this eccentric hilltop park. Sadly, Eusebi Güell's plan to create a residential garden city here, with 60 houses set in formal gardens, never came to fruition and the park was deemed a failure in its day. Only two houses were built, including the one where Gaudí briefly lived (now the Casa Museu Gaudí, containing a small but moving selection of his personal artefacts, wrought-ironwork and items of furniture).

Today, Parc Güell is considered one of the city's treasures, outstanding for its clever fusion of architectural elements into the landscaping. In 1969, it was declared a national monument. Throughout its 20 ha (49 acres), there are surreal sculptures, steps, bridges, and paths raised on columns of 'dripping' stonework. The main entrance is especially impressive, with massive wrought-iron gates, flanked by two oval pavilions with colourful mosaic domes.

⬤ *The curvaceous main entrance to Parc Güell*

From here, a grand stairway, ornamented by a mosaic salamander fountain, leads to the Sala Hipòstila, a vast cavernous space originally intended as the marketplace. Its circular rooftop plaza, supported by 86 Doric columns, is edged with a curved continuous bench covered in multi-coloured *trencadís* (broken ceramics). The plaza affords far-reaching city vistas and makes an ideal picnic spot. ❷ Carrer d'Olot (park); Carretera del Carmel (museum) ❶ 932 130 488 (park); 932 193 811 (museum) ◐ 10.00–18.00 Mar–Oct; 10.00–19.00 Apr–Sept (museum) ❷ Bus 24, 25

Plaça de Catalunya

This busy square is the nerve-centre of Barcelona, at the confluence of many major thoroughfares: La Rambla and Avinguda del Portal de l'Angel to the south; and Passeig de Gràcia and La Rambla de Catalunya to the north. The square adopted its final form in the 1920s, when an extensive esplanade was added to join the Old Town with the Eixample, and the square replaced Plaça de Sant Jaume as the heart of Barcelona. Today, with its sculptures and symmetrical fountains, it is a central meeting point for Barcelonans, and a popular place for children to feed the pigeons.

CULTURE

Fundació Antoni Tàpies (Antoni Tàpies Foundation)

Catalan artist Antoni Tàpies founded the Tàpies Foundation in 1984 to promote the study and understanding of modern art. It contains a specialist library, which documents art and artists of the 20th century, and one of the most extensive collections of Tàpies' own paintings, drawings and sculptures. It also hosts temporary exhibitions.

The Foundation is housed in a particularly unusual building, built in the 1880s by Lluís Domènech i Montaner, and it is considered to be the initiator of the Modernist movement. The imposing Mudejar-style façade is crowned by an eye-catching wire sculpture *Cloud and Chair*, made by Tapìes in 1990, which has since become a symbol of the Foundation and the city.

ⓐ Carrer d'Aragó 255 ❶ 934 870 315 ⓦ www.fundaciotapies.org
ⓔ museu@ftapies.com ❺ 10.00–20.00 Tues–Sun ⓝ Metro: Passeig de Gràcia

RETAIL THERAPY

Fashion
Adolfo Dominguez One of Spain's top menswear designers, famed for making linen suits popular with the slogan 'wrinkles are fashionable'. ⓐ Passeig de Gràcia 89 ❶ 932 151 339
ⓦ www.adolfodominguez.com ⓝ Metro: Passeig de Gràcia

Antonio Miró A local designer, celebrated worldwide for his shoes, spectacles and furnishings as well as his fashions for men, women and children. ⓐ Carrer Consell de Cent 349 ❶ 934 870 670
ⓦ www.antoniomiro.es ⓝ Metro: Passeig de Gràcia

Bagúes One of the world's leading Modernist jewellers, housed in Casa Amatller (see page 90). ⓐ Passeig de Gràcia 41 ❶ 932 160 174
ⓝ Metro: Passeig de Gràcia

Muxart Fantastic creations by flamboyant Barcelonan shoe designer, Hermenegildo Muxart. ⓐ Carrer Roselló 230 ❶ 934 871 591
ⓦ www.muxart.com ⓝ Metro: Provença or Diagonal

Gifts & design

BD Ediciones de Diseno Innovative furniture and avant-garde home design, beautifully displayed in a *Modernista* house. ⓐ Carrer Mallorca 291–3 ⓣ 932 080 345 ⓦ www.bdbarcelona.com
Ⓜ Metro: Diagonal

Dos i Una Barcelona's first design shop is full of state-of-the-art gadgetry and amusing gift ideas. ⓐ Carrer Rossello 275 ⓣ 932 177 032
Ⓜ Metro: Diagonal

Puzzlemanía Over 1,000 jigsaws for the amusement of young and old. ⓐ Carrer Diputació 225 ⓣ 934 515 803 Ⓜ Metro: Universitat

Vinçon A trendy home design 'department store'. ⓐ Passeig de Gracià 96 ⓣ 932 156 050 ⓦ www.vincon.com Ⓜ Metro: Passeig de Gracià

TAKING A BREAK

Bodega Sepúlveda £ ❶ The speciality at this genuine locals' bar is *boquerones* (fresh anchovies). ⓐ Carrer Sepúlveda 173 ⓣ 323 59 44
Ⓛ Closed Sat morning & Sun Ⓜ Metro: Universitat

Qu-Qu £–££ ❷ A delicatessen-cum-tapas bar, serving delicious Catalan cheeses and cold cuts. ⓐ Passeig de Gràcia 24 ⓣ 933 174 512
ⓦ www.angrup.com Ⓜ Metro: Passeig de Gràcia

Flash-flash Tortilleria ££ ❸ *Tortillas* (omlettes) and salad – perfect for a light lunch in Gràcia. ⓐ Carrer Granada del Penedès 25 ⓣ 932 370 990 Ⓛ 11.00–02.00 Ⓜ Metro: Diagonal

Valentin ££ ❹ Delicious cold meats and sausages at a specialist *xarcuteria*. Try a portion of *chorizo*, *salchichón* or *bellota* ham. ⓐ Carrer de la Diputació 301 ❶ 934 872 372 Ⓝ Metro: Passeig de Gràcia

AFTER DARK

Restaurants
El Glop £ ❺ Try the char-grilled meat dishes at this popular affordable restaurant. The local wines are good too. ⓐ Rambla Catalunya 65 ❶ 934 870 097 ❶ Closed Mon Ⓝ Metro: Passeig de Gràcia

Noti ££ ❻ Creative Spanish-Italian cuisine in a sleek, urban interior – a popular choice for business lunches. ⓐ Carrer Roger de Llúria 35 ❶ 933 426 673 Ⓝ Metro: Passeig de Gràcia

Beltxenea £££ ❼ Exceptional Basque cuisine in a stylish *Modernismo* setting. ⓐ Carrer de Mallorca 275 ❶ 932 153 024 ❶ Closed Sat lunch & Sun Ⓝ Metro: Diagonal

Jean Luc Figueras £££ ❽ One of Barcelona's several Michelin-starred restaurants, serving seasonal Catalan cuisine in a luxurious townhouse in Gràcia. ⓐ Carrer Santa Teresa 10 ❶ 934 152 877 Ⓦ www.jeanlucfigueras.com ❶ Closed Sun Ⓝ Metro: Diagonal

Bars, clubs & live music
La Bolsa Play the market at 'the Stock Exchange' where the drink prices, shown on computer screens, fluctuate according to a drink's popularity that night. Good fun! ⓐ Carrer Tuset 17 ❶ 934 202 635 Ⓝ Metro: Passeig de Gràcia

Distrito Diagonal See and be seen with the Eixample's beautiful people in this laid-back bar and nightclub. ⓐ Avinguda Diagonal 442 ⓣ 934 154 635 ⓛ from 22.00 Wed–Sun ⓜ Metro: Diagonal

Nick Havanna This long-running club remains hugely popular, thanks to its sensational design and wide choice of music from hip-hop and house to hit parade. ⓐ Carrer Roselló 208 ⓣ 932 17 732 ⓦ www.nickhavanna.net ⓛ midnight–06.00 ⓜ Metro: Diagonal

Otto Zutz A three-storey converted warehouse with eight bars and three dance floors offering house music, funk, hip-hop and soul sounds. ⓐ Carrer Lincoln 15 ⓣ 932 380 722 ⓦ www.grupo-ottozutz.com ⓛ 23.00–06.00 Tues–Sat ⓜ Metro: Fontana or Passeig de Gràcia

Xampanyería Casablanca A champagne bar fashioned after the Bogart-Bergman film, which serves four kinds of house *cava* by the glass, accompanied by tasty tapas snacks. ⓐ Carrer Bonavista 6 ⓣ 932 376 399 ⓛ 18.30–02.30 Thur–Sun, 18.30–03.00 Fri & Sat ⓜ Metro: Passeig de Gràcia

Theatre, music & dance
Centre Artesà Tradicionàrius (CAT) Founded in 1993, the Tradicionàrius is devoted to the study, teaching and performance of Catalan traditional music and dance. ⓐ Travessera de Sant Antoní 6–8 ⓣ 932 184 485 ⓦ www.tradicionarius.com ⓜ Metro: Fontana

Montjuïc & El Raval

South of the city, the vast hill of Montjuïc is named 'Mountain of the Jews' after an early Jewish necropolis here. In 1929 it was the venue for the International Expo, and in 1992 it was the main site of the Barcelona Olympics. Today, with its top-notch sports facilities, together with some of the city's finest museums and galleries, it is a popular place for both locals and visitors at weekends. On the lower slopes of Montjuïc, the up-and-coming residential *barri* (quarter) of Poble Sec was once so poor it didn't even have a water supply, hence its name – 'Dry Village'. It joins the lively district of El Raval, also known as Barri Xinès (China Town), formerly a run-down area renowned as a centre of drugs, crime and prostitution. Nowadays, it has tidied up its act and, thanks to the opening of such institutions as the Museum of Contemporary Art (MACBA) and the neighbouring Contemporary Cultural Centre (CCCB), it is becoming newly fashionable.

SIGHTS & ATTRACTIONS

L'Anella Olímpica (The Olympic Ring)

A space-age communications tower dominates the skyline on Montjuïc hill. It marks the Olympic Ring – a monumental sports complex of concrete and marble which served, in 1992, as the main venue for the Olympic Games. The Estadi Olímpic (Olympic Stadium) was originally designed in 1936 as an alternative venue to the Nazis' infamous Berlin Games, but these were cancelled on the outbreak of Civil War, just one day before the official opening. Today, highlights of the 1992 Games can be relived though memorabilia and video clippings in the Galería Olímpica, situated beneath the

stadium. Also open to the public are the Picornell outdoor swimming pool and the state-of-the-art domed Palau Sant Jordi, which looks more like a UFO than an indoor sports arena.
ⓐ Avinguda de l'Estadi/Passeig Olímpic, Montjuïc ⓣ 934 260 660 (Galería Olímpica) ⓦ www.fundaciobarcelonaolimpica.es
ⓔ fbo@fundaciobarcelonaolimpica.es ⓛ 10.00–14.00, 16.00–19.00 Mon–Fri, Apr–Sept; 10.00–13.00, 16.00–18.00 Mon–Fri, Oct–Mar (Galería Olímpica) ⓝ Bus 50

Castell de Montjuïc (Montjuïc Castle)

This imposing 18th-century fortress, standing on the bluff of Montjuïc hill, was built by the Spanish to stop the people of Barcelona from rebelling. Inside, the **Museu Militar** (Military Museum) contains an impressive collection of weaponry, maps, lead soldiers and uniforms. The bird's-eye views from the battlements are breathtaking.
ⓐ Avinguda del Castell, Montjuïc ⓣ 933 298 613 ⓛ 09.30–17.30 Nov–mid-Mar; 09.30–20.00 mid-Mar–Oct ⓝ Funicular Telefèric de Montjuc; Bus 50

Palau Güell (Güell Palace)

This eccentric building, constructed in the 1880s, was Antoni Gaudí's first major architectural project. It was commissioned by the affluent industrialist Eusebi Güell, who shocked society by announcing he wished to move into Carrer Nou de la Rambla, on the fringe of El Raval's notorious red-light district, rather than the fashionable new Eixample district, in order to be near his parents' home on La Rambla. Given the seedy neighbourhood, Gaudí created an austere façade

◀ *The striking Torre de Calatrava at l'Anella Olímpica*

107

resembling a fortress, with battlements, grilles like portcullises and wrought-iron dragons to fend off unwanted visitors.

The interior is lavishly decorated and fascinating. Follow the one-hour guided tour down to the cavernous basement stables, through various rooms decorated with *Modernista* furniture and fittings of wrought-iron, glass, ceramics and wood, and up to the rooftop terrace – an extraordinary forest of quirky finials and chimneys, decorated with coloured *trencadis* mosaics (broken ceramic pieces) and glass. The Güell family did not live here long as the palace was confiscated by Spanish Civil War anarchists in 1936, who used it as their military headquarters and prison. Today, it is protected as a UNESCO World Heritage Site.

ⓐ Carrer Nou de la Rambla ⓣ 933 173 974 ⓛ 10.00–18.00 Mon–Sat (guided tours only)

Pavelló Barcelona (Barcelona Pavilion)

This masterpiece of modern rationalist design was created on the lower slopes of Montjuic Hill for the 1929 International Expo by the celebrated Bauhaus architect Ludwig Mies van der Rohe, dismantled at the end of the fair and subsequently reconstructed in the 1980s to commemorate the centenary of his birth. It is a construction of astonishing simplicity, combining marble, oynx, glass, chrome and water using simple geometrical forms and clean lines. Its ultra-minimalist functional interior contains an exhibition on the architect's life and work, and includes his famous square-shaped leather-and-steel 'Barcelona Chair', created especially for the exhibition, which has since become an icon of modern design.

ⓐ Avinguda del Marquès de Comillas, Montjuïc ⓣ 934 234 016 ⓦ www.miesbcn.com ⓔ pavello@miesbcn.com ⓛ 10.00–20.00 ⓝ Bus 13, 50 & 100

MONTJUÏC & EL RAVAL

Plaça d'Espanya

This bustling square and major traffic intersection was originally designed as a grand entrance to the 1929 Universal Exposition. The square itself is dominated by a classical-style fountain. There is a sound and light show during the summer. The unusual Moorish-style building on one corner is the former bullring. It backs onto the windswept **Parc Joan Miró** (Joan Miro Park), with its startling 22 m (72 ft) high mosaic sculpture entitled *Dona i Ocell* (Woman and Bird).

Back in Plaça d'Espanya, a series of staircases, fountains and outdoor escalators leads you towards the impressive Palau Nacional and MNAC (see page 112). But the real crowd-puller is **La Font Màgica** (The Magic Fountain), Montjuïc's nightly illuminated, musical fountain displays in summer.

ⓐ Plaça Espanya Ⓜ Metro: Espanya

Poble Espanyol (Spanish Village)

This purpose-built 'Spanish Village' was originally conceived as a whistle-stop tour of the nation for the 1929 Universal Exposition. Today it remains a hugely popular showcase of regional architecture with 117 life-sized reproductions of famous or characteristic buildings, six squares and 3 km (2 miles) of streets. Also within the village are bars and restaurants serving regional specialities, and studios demonstrating local craft-making skills. On Sundays at midday a *festa* enlivens the main square.

ⓐ Avinguda del Marquès de Comillas 13, Montjuïc ❶ 935 086 300
ⓦ www.poble-espanyol.com ⓔ info@poble-espanyol.com
🕐 09.00–20.00 Mon, 09.00–02.00 Tues–Thur, 09.00–04.00 Fri–Sat, 09.00–24.00 Sun, Mar–Dec; 09.00–20.00 Mon–Thur, 09.00–04.00 Fri–Sat, 09.00–24.00 Sun, Jan–Feb Ⓜ Metro: Espanya; Bus 13 & 50

CULTURE

Fundació Joan Miró (Joan Miró Foundation)

Fundació Joan Miró, on Montjuïc hill, pays homage to one of Barcelona's greatest artists. Famous for his childlike style and use of vivid primary colours, his work captures the very essence of this vibrant Mediterranean city. Miró was born in Barcelona in 1893 and spent most of his life here, developing his bold childlike style and use of bright vibrant colours. The gallery, itself a work of art designed by Josep Lluís Sert, is a beautiful modern building of airy white spaces, massive windows and skylights set in gardens overlooking the city – and a perfect backdrop for 240 paintings, 175 sculptures, around 8,000 drawings, nine tapestries, four ceramics and his complete graphic works – the most complete collection of Miró's work in the world, many of which were donated to the Foundation by Miró himself.

The Foundation also stages temporary exhibitions of modern art, contemporary music recitals and a special permanent exhibition entitled 'To Joan Miró', including works by Calder, Ernst, Tàpies, Moore, Matisse and others, given to the Foundation in memory of the great Catalan surrealist.

ⓐ Avinguda de Miramar, Montjuïc ❶ 934 439 470
ⓦ www.bcn.fjmiro.es ⓔ fjmiro@bcn.fjmiro.es ❶ 10.00–19.00 Tues–Sat (until 21.00 Thur), 10.00–14.30 Sun, closed Mon, Oct–June; 10.00–20.00 Tues–Sat (until 21.30 Thur), 10.00–14.30 Sun, closed Mon, July–Sept ❷ Bus 50 or 55

◀ *Sculpture – and a great view – at the Fundació Joan Miró*

Museu d'Art Contemporani de Barcelona – MACBA (Museum of Contemporary Art)

Hidden amid the shabby narrow backstreets in El Raval, this dazzling white glass-fronted museum comes as a surprise, towering over the stark concrete Plaça dels Àngels. The dramatic building, with its swooping ramps, white-on-white décor and glass-walled galleries designed by American architect Richard Meier, was initially the subject of much controversy and almost upstages the art installations which it contains. Nonetheless, it is regarded as one of the city's must-see galleries, focusing on the art movements of the second half of the 20th century, with special emphasis on Catalan and Spanish artists. Its extensive collection is exhibited in rotation, with works by Klee, Tàpies, Miró, Calder and Hurst among others. It also hosts temporary contemporary art exhibitions.

Plaça dels Àngels 1 ✆ 934 120 810 🌐 www.macba.es ✉ macba@macba.es 🕐 11.00–19.30 Mon, Wed–Fri, 10.00–20.00 Sat, 10.00–15.00 Sun, closed Tues Ⓝ Metro: Catalunya

Museu Nacional d'Art de Catalunya – MNAC (National Art Museum of Catalonia)

The staggering collections of the MNAC span a thousand years of Catalan art, from the 10th to the 20th centuries. They are housed in an imposing neoclassical palace, the Palau Nacional. Originally built as the symbol of the 1929 World Exhibition, it has recently been renovated by architect Gae Aulenti (who converted the Gare d'Orsay into one of Paris's foremost museums).

Among the MNAC's numerous treasures is one of the finest collections of medieval art in the world, divided into Romanesque and Gothic. The idea for this collection originated in the early 20th century, when theft of national architectural treasures was rife in

Catalonia. The Romanesque Galleries trace the evolution of Catalan Romanesque art through a remarkable series of 11th- and 12th-century murals carefully stripped from the apses of churches throughout the region, and each painstakingly reconstructed in situ as if they were still in their original venues. There is also an impressive display of stone sculptures, wood carvings, gold and silverwork, altar cloths, enamels and coins. In contrast to the simplicity of the Romanesque style, the colourful Gothic collection presents over 400 highly ornate retables and sculptures, including an extraordinary 15th-century Virgin in full flamenco dress.

⬤ *The dramatic MACBA (Museum of Contemporary Art) building*

The Renaissance and baroque art section includes part of the dazzling Thyssen-Bornemisza Collection, formerly housed in Pedralbes Monastery (see page 125), containing predominantly 13th- to 18th-century Italian and German paintings, including works by Fra Angélico, Titian, Rubens, Canaletto and Velázquez.

The modern art collection is considered the most important ensemble of Catalan art from the 19th and early 20th centuries. It starts with works by Maria Fortuny, the earliest of the *Modernistas* and the first Catalan artist to be widely known abroad, through the less adventurous *Noucentista* (Noucentisme) movement and Impressionism to the avant-garde. The sculptures here are especially notable. However, the highlight of this collection is its decorative arts – a magnificent array of jewellery, textiles, stained glass and ceramics by such leading exponents of the era as Cadafalch and Gaudí.

The museum also includes an interesting display of photography, from its origins to the present day, and an important collection of coins, medals and papers from the 6th century BC to the present day.

ⓐ Palau Nacional, Montjuïc ❶ 936 220 376 ⓦ www.mnac.es ⓔ mnac@mnac.es ⓛ 10.00–19.00 Tues–Sat, 10.00–14.30 Sun, closed Mon ⓜ Metro: Espanya

Museu Marítim (Maritime Museum)

The Maritime Museum is housed in the magnificent **Drassanes Reials** (Royal Shipyards), the largest and most complete medieval dockyards in the world. These impressive boatyards were built in the 13th century, at the height of Catalonia's maritime power, and are a triumph of Gothic civic architecture. Maps, charts, compasses, paintings, model ships, figureheads and countless other treasures of Barcelona's lengthy seafaring past fill their vast, church-like, stone-vaulted halls, and there are polyglot audio-guides to steer visitors around the key attractions.

Numerous boats are also on show, from the gold-medal-winning Flying Dutchman sloop raced by the Spanish sailing team at the Barcelona Olympics to a 60 m (197 ft) replica of the royal galley *La Real*, flagship of Don Juan of Austria, which forms part of an exciting 45-minute multimedia spectacle 'The Great Sea Adventure'. The museum's flagship, the early 20th-century three-masted schooner *Santa Eulàlia* (renamed in honour of Barcelona's patron saint) has recently been restored. She is moored at the wooden pier at Barcelona's old port and is now also open to the public.
ⓐ Avinguda de les Drassanes ① 933 429 920
ⓦ www.museumaritimbarcelona.org ⓔ m.maritim@diba.es
🕑 Museum: 10.00–20.00. Schooner: 12.00–19.30 Tues–Fri, 10.00–19.00 Sat & Sun, May–Oct; 12.00–17.30 Tues–Fri, 10.00–17.00 Sat & Sun, Nov–Apr ⓜ Metro: Drassanes

RETAIL THERAPY

Considering the number of tourist attractions, this area is surprisingly devoid of boutiques. However, several museum shops (including MACBA, MNAC and Fundació Miró) stock a high-quality selection of designer items, books, gifts and arty souvenirs inspired by their collections.

Poble Espanyol Around 40 art and craft workshops in a reproduction 'Spanish Village' (see page 109), selling wood-carvings, glassware, jewellery, ceramics, puppets and leatherwares from all corners of the nation, alongside the more touristic but fun flamenco costumes, guitars, fans and castanets. ⓐ Avinguda Marqués de Comillas 13 ① 935 086 300 ⓦ www.poble-espanyol.com 🕑 09.00–20.00 Mon,

09.00–02.00 Tues–Thur, 09.00–04.00 Fri & Sat, 09.00–24.00 Sun,
Mar–Dec; 09.00–20.00 Mon–Thur, 09.00–04.00 Fri & Sat,
09.00–24.00 Sun, Jan & Feb ⓜ Metro: Espanya; Bus 13, 50

TAKING A BREAK

Albi £ ❶ One of several restaurants in the Poble Espanyol (see
page 109), this one serves simple Catalan rice, fish and meat dishes
on a shady terrace overlooking the main square. ⓐ Casa del Cabildo,
Poble Espanyol ⓣ 934 249 324 ⓦ www.restaurantalbi.com ⓜ Metro:
Espanya; Bus 13, 50

Biocenter £ ❷ Barcelona has only a handful of vegetarian
restaurants, and this is one of the best, serving delicious soups,
salads and casseroles. ⓐ Carrer Pintor Fortuny 25 ⓣ 933 014 583
ⓛ 12.00–24.00 ⓜ Metro: Plaça de Catalunya

Garduña £ ❸ One of the most popular restaurants in the
immediate vicinity of La Boqueria market (see page 68), serving
super fresh food in simple surrounds. The seafood platters are
especially good, and the *menú del dia* (menu of the day) is
always excellent value. ⓐ Carrer Jerusalem 18 ⓣ 933 024 323
ⓦ www.lagardunya.com ⓛ Closed Sun evening ⓜ Metro: Liceu

AFTER DARK

Restaurants
La Bella Napoli £ ❹ This jolly restaurant serves some of the best
pizzas in town. ⓐ Carrer de Margarit 14 ⓣ 934 425 056 ⓛ Closed
Mon ⓜ Metro: Paral.lel or Poble Sec

L'Eucaliptus £ ❺ A tiny, tiled restaurant just off La Rambla,
serving a simple but delicious choice of *escalivada* (Catalan-style
ratatouille), asparagus, tacos and *torradas* (open sandwiches).
ⓐ Carrer Bonsuccés 4 ⓣ 933 021 824 Ⓜ Metro: Catalunya

🔺 *Take your pick from the menu of the day*

Ca L'isidre £££ ⑥ Despite its downmarket location in Poble Sec, this small bastion of contemporary Mediterranean cuisine counts King Juan Carlos among its regulars. ⓐ Carrer Les Flors 12 ❶ 934 411 139 ⓦ www.calisidre.com ❶ Closed Sun ⓝ Metro: Paral.lel

Quo Vadis £££ ⑦ Classic Spanish cuisine near the Liceu theatre (see page 65). There's even a special post-theatre menu. ⓐ Carrer del Carme 7 ❶ 933 024 072 ⓦ www.restaurantquovadis.com ❶ Closed Sun ⓝ Metro: Liceu

Bars, clubs & live music

Club Sala Apolo This lively club, in an elegant old ballroom in the Poble Sec district, caters for all tastes and ages, with African, Latin and Spanish music, live bands and, at weekends, the popular DJ team Nitsa. ⓐ Carrer Nou de la Rambla 113 ❶ 934 414 001 ⓦ www.sala-apolo.com ⓝ Metro: Paral.lel

Estadi Olímpic The main venue for mega-star pop concerts, together with neighbouring Palau Sant Jordi. Tickets are best obtained through record shops. ⓐ Avinguda de l'Estadi ❶ 934 260 660 ⓝ Bus 13, 50

La Paloma Hugely popular club in a *Modernista* dance hall complete with faded drapes, gilt angels and crystal chandeliers, with music from funky house to Latin vibe. ⓐ Carrer Tigre 27 ❶ 933 016 897 ⓦ www.lapaloma-bcn.com ❶ 23.30–05.30 ⓝ Metro: Universitat

Pastis A tiny rustic bar with a bohemian atmosphere redolent of Paris's Latin Quarter. ⓐ Carrer Santa Mònica 4 ❶ 318 79 80 ❶ 19.30–02.30 ⓝ Metro: Drassanes

La Terrazza Dance till dawn under the stars to house and techno music at this summertime open-air club. ⓐ Avinguda Muntanyans, Montjuïc ⏰ 24.00–06.00 Fri–Sat, May–Oct Ⓝ Bus 13, 50

Torres de Ávila One of Barcelona's most celebrated designer bars, with stunning rooftop terraces, and all-night trance-techno discos on summer weekends. ⓐ Avinguda Marquès de Comillas, Poble Espanyol, Montjuïc ☎ 934 249 309 Ⓝ Bus 13, 50

Culture
Centre de Cultura Contemporània de Barcelona (CCCB) This new arts centre, in a strikingly converted 19th-century workhouse, stages a wide variety of performance arts, including concerts, theatre, dance and film. ⓐ Carrer del Montalegre 5 ☎ 933 064 100 Ⓦ www.cccb.org Ⓝ Metro: Catalunya

Fundació Joan Miró The Miró Foundation (see page 111) contains Spain's chief centre for contemporary music development. It stages frequent concerts including the *Nits de Música* series in June and July. ⓐ Avinguda de Miramar, Parc de Montjuïc ☎ 934 439 470 Ⓦ www.bcn.fjmiro.es Ⓝ Bus 50, 55

El Tablao de Carmen The flamenco shows here are touristic but fun. Advance booking is essential. ⓐ Poble Espanyol, Montjuïc ☎ 933 256 895 Ⓦ www.tablaodecarmen.com Ⓝ Bus 13, 50

Pedralbes, Tibidabo & Les Corts

Pedralbes and Tibidabo are part of Barcelona's Zona Alta (Upper Zone), at a slightly higher elevation than the city centre. These smart hilly suburbs have been popular residential areas for centuries, with beautiful villas, gardens and parks draped over their hillsides. The area also contains some elegant restaurants and bars, but surprisingly few shops.

At 550 m (1,800 ft), Mont Tibidabo, part of the Collserola range, forms the northwestern boundary of Barcelona. Pedralbes is situated at the top of the Avinguda Diagonal to the northwest of the city centre, and contains a beautiful medieval monastery and a Royal Palace with impressive ceramic and decorative arts collections. Immediately south of Pedralbes, the once rural *barri* of Les Corts (The Farmsheds), contains the stadium and museum of Barça, Barcelona's remarkable football team.

SIGHTS & ATTRACTIONS

Museu del Futbol Club Barcelona (Museum of FC Barcelona)

If you can't get a ticket for a match, at least visit this – one of the city's most popular museums – and stand on the terraces of the second largest football stadium in the world (after Rio's Maracanã), with seating capacity for 120,000 fans. Barcelona is football-crazy and FC Barça is one of Catalonia's flagship institutions. Not only is it the fifth most successful business in Spain, but it is also the richest sports club in the world, with the largest membership of any soccer club.

The museum is under the terraces at Entrance 9, and contains a dazzling display of trophies, strips, photographic archives, audiovisual shows of famous match highlights and an impressive

range of memorabilia documenting the history of football from its origins until the present day and, in particular, this club's extraordinary history as a political vehicle and as a rallying point for Catalans.

ⓐ Camp Nou – Estadi FCB (accesos 9), Avinguda Arístides Maillol
ⓣ 934 963 600 ⓦ www.fcbarcelona.com
ⓔ museu@club.fcbarcelona.com ⓛ 10.00–18.30 (stadium until 17.30) Mon–Sat, 10.00–14.30 (stadium until 13.30) Sun; 10.00–13.00 on match days (no stadium visits) ⓜ Metro: Collblanc

Finca Güell

Every well-to-do member of the Barcelonan middle classes had a *finca* (country house) or a *torre* (villa) in the countryside at the turn of the 20th century and, as a consequence, the Zona Alta area is dotted with fine *Modernista* buildings. One such gem is Finca Güell, former holiday estate of the wealthy Güell family, ardent patrons of Antoni Gaudí. Today the building houses La Càtedra Gaudí, an institution specialising in subjects connected with this famous architect. Although the main buildings are closed to the public, it is still possible to admire his elaborate Moorish-style gatehouses and extraordinary gates depicting a dragon – a veritable masterpiece of *Modernisme* wrought-ironwork.

ⓐ Avinguda de Pedralbes 7 ⓣ 932 045 250 ⓛ 09.00–13.00 ⓜ Metro: Palau Reial

Serra de Collserola (Collserola Range)

The hills of the Collserola range lie to the north and west of the city, forming a wonderful 6,550 ha (16,185 acres) nature reserve with extensive woodlands full of wildlife and meadows ablaze with wild flowers. Walking here is easy, as the paths and climbs are well maintained, with clearly defined picnic areas. This area is best accessed by taking an FGC train to Baixador de Vallvidrera, from where it is a short walk to the **information centre**, where details of walks and cycle routes are available. Nearby, British architect Norman Foster's glass-and-steel 268 m (879 ft) communications tower, the **Torre de Collserola** (Collserola Tower), whisks those with a head for heights up to an observation platform by glass-fronted lift for the most sensational views over the city and, on exceptionally clear days, as far as Mallorca.

ⓐ Centre d'Informacio, Parc de Collserola ❶ 932 803 552
🕒 09.30–15.00 Ⓜ FGC Baixador de Vallvidrera

Tibidabo

Tibidabo is the highest peak of the Collserola range and the biggest draw for Barcelonans, who come especially at weekends to enjoy the superb views and the **Parc d'Atraccions**, an old-fashioned fairground of carousels, bumper cars, a hall of mirrors and a Ferris wheel, combined with a handful of more high-tech attractions. Getting there, on an ancient tram and then by funicular, is all part of a fun family day out. No wonder locals nickname it La Muntanya Màgica (The Magic Mountain). Here too, the **Museu d'Autòmats del Tibidabo** contains a splendid collection of coin-operated fairground machines dating from the early 20th century. The modern **Temple Expiatori** (Church of Atonement) crowns the summit of Tibidabo – a neo-Gothic fantasy topped by a massive statue of Christ.

ⓐ Parc d'Atraccions, Plaça del Tibidabo 3–4 ❶ 932 117 942
Ⓦ www.tibidabo.es ⓔ tibidabo@tibidabo.es 🕒 10.00–19.00/20.00, late Mar–early Oct; 12.00–22.00/23.00, July–Aug; 12.00–18.00 Sat & Sun only (winter) Ⓜ FGC Avinguda del Tibidabo, plus Tramvia Blau and Funicular

Tramvía Blau (Blue Tram)

The electric Tramvía Blau is one of the last vestiges of the city's tram system, in operation since 1902, and a true symbol of Barcelona's identity. It rattles along Avinguda Tibidabo between the FGC station and Plaça Doctor Andreu, passing many fine *Modernista* houses en route. At the end of the journey, take a table on the terrace of La Venta (see page 127). Then, take the **Funicular de Tibidabo** from here to the Parc d'Atraccions (see page 123) at Tibidabo's peak.

CULTURE

Cosmocaixa Barcelona

The city's state-of-the-art science museum is located at the foot of Mont Collserola. It is divided into a number of sections including: The Geological Wall (illustrating the world's geology); Science Square (an open-air space full of hands-on scientific experiments); a Planetarium; a Bubble Planetarium ('child-size astronomy', aimed at 3–8-year-olds);

○ *Take a trip on the electric Tramvia Blau*

and the Flooded Forest (the first flooded Amazonian forest on display inside a science museum). This fascinating new centre is a must for budding scientists young and old.

ⓐ Carrer Teodor Roviralta 47–51 ⓣ 932 126 050
ⓦ www.cosmocaixa.com ⓔ info.fundacio@lacaixa.es
ⓛ 10.00–20.00 Tues–Sun, closed Mon ⓜ FGC Avinguda Tibidabo and then Tramvía Blau

Monestir de Pedralbes (Pedralbes Monastery)

This exquisite monastery was founded in 1326 by the Catalan King Jaume II and Queen Elisenda de Montcada for the nuns of the St Clare of Assisi order. The King died in 1327, just two years after their marriage, and Queen Elisenda spent the remaining 37 years of her life here. The Montcadas were among the most powerful families of their day and, under her auspices, the monastery grew rich and flourished. Today the monastery is still used by a small community of Clarista nuns.

The monastery takes its name from the Latin *petrae albae* (white stones), best seen in the elegant three-storey cloisters, which count among the city's finest medieval treasures. Enjoy the tranquillity of the central courtyard, fragrant with flowers and medicinal herbs, before visiting the refectory, chapter house, the Queen's grave and a series of beautifully painted prayer cells. Don't miss the Capella de

WHAT'S IN A NAME?

The name 'Tibidabo' comes from the words uttered by Satan during his temptation of Christ in the wilderness: '*Haec omnia tibi dabo* (all these things will I give to you), *si cadens adoraberis me* (if thou wilt fall down and worship me)'.

Sant Miquel (St Michael's Cell), with its impressive 14th-century frescoes depicting the life of the Virgin and the Passion.

ⓐ Baixada del Monastir 9 ❶ 932 039 282 ❷ 10.00–14.00 Tues–Sun

Palau Reial de Pedralbes (Royal Palace of Pedralbes)

In 1919 the handsome villa of Can Feliu was converted into a royal residence for the King of Spain for the 1929 International Exhibition. After 1939, it was Franco's city residence and, following a handful of subsequent visits by royalty and heads of state, it was opened to the public in 1960. The impressive state rooms contain two museums. The **Museu de les Arts Decoratives** (Decorative Arts Museum) has an eclectic display of artefacts spanning the early Middle Ages to the present day, with special emphasis on the 20th century, most notably Modernism, Functionalism and Minimalism. The **Museu de la Ceràmica** (Ceramic Museum) traces Spanish ceramics from the 12th century, arranged by regional styles. Look out especially for the beautiful Catalan baroque panels *La Xocolatada* (The Chocolate Party) showing chocolate-drinking at a garden party, and the atmospheric *La Cursa de Braus* (The Bullfight), as well as the impressive pieces by Miró and Picasso.

The landscaped grounds make a lovely picnic venue, and there is even a fountain by Gaudí.

ⓐ Av. Diagonal 686 ❶ 932 801 621 ❷ 10.00–18.00 Tues–Sat, 10.00–15.00 Sun ❻ Metro: Palau Reial

RETAIL THERAPY

There are very few shops in this part of town. However, these two shopping centres should cater for most needs:

El Corte Inglés A branch of the city's foremost department store, selling everything from designer fashions to electronics, books, toys, jewellery and cosmetics. There is also a full supermarket, cáfeteria and restaurant. ⓐ Avinguda Diagonal 617 ⓣ 933 667 100 ⓦ www.elcorteingles.es ⓜ Metro: Maria Christina

Pedralbes Centre This shopping centre, next door to El Corte Inglés, contains a wide variety of fashion, shoe, jewellery and design boutiques, including such names as Mango, Timberland and Armani Casa. There are also a handful of eateries and, during winter months, the square outside is turned into an ice rink. ⓐ Avinguda Diagonal 609–15 ⓣ 934 106 821 ⓦ www.pedralbescentre.com ⓜ Metro: Maria Christina

TAKING A BREAK

La Venta £–££ ❶ This delightful Moorish-style open-air café at the foot of the Tibidabo funicular, with its glass conservatory and outdoor terrace, is the ideal venue for lunch or some light refreshment. ⓐ Plaça Doctor Andreu ⓣ 932 126 455 ⓛ Closed Sun ⓜ FGC Avinguda Tibidabo then Tramvia Blau

AFTER DARK

Restaurants
La Balsa ££ ❷ Enjoy top-notch Catalan, Basque and Mediterranean cuisine accompanied by bird's-eye views of the city, served atop a circular tower originally built as a water cistern, near the science museum. ⓐ Carrer Infanta Isabel 4 ⓣ 932 115 048 ⓛ Closed Mon lunch & all day Sun ⓜ FGC Avinguda del Tibidabo

127

Neichel £££ ❸ Located at the heart of Pedralbes, this is one of the city's finest restaurants, thanks to Alsace-born chef Jean-Louis Neichel, who boasts the accolade 'the most brilliant ambassador French cuisine has ever had within Spain'. ⓐ Carrer Beltran y Rózpide 1–5 ❶ 932 038 408 ⓦ www.neichel.es ⓛ Closed Sat lunch & all day Sun ⓝ Palau Reial

Bars, clubs & live music
Danzatoria This fine mansion on the slopes of Tibidabo offers Barcelona's beautiful people four floors with different types of music (house, lounge, pop and chill out), rambling gardens and a huge terrace. ⓐ Avinguda Tibidabo 61 ❶ 211 62 61 ⓦ www.danzatoria-barcelona.com ⓛ 19.00–03.00 Tue–Sun ⓝ FGC Avinguda Tibidabo

Mirablau The chic set enjoy this stylish bar and garden terrace on Mont Tibidabo, with its spectacular views over the city and the port. It is especially romantic at dusk when the city lights start to twinkle. ⓐ Plaça Doctor Andreu ❶ 934 185 879 ⓝ FGC Avinguda Tibidabo then Tramvia Blau

Tres Torres This sophisticated *Modernista* mansion with beautiful gardens, terrace, cocktail lounge and discotheque attracts a classy clientele to its elegant surroundings. On some nights there is live jazz or blues. ⓐ Via Augusta 300 ❶ 205 16 08 ⓛ 17.00–03.00 ⓝ FGC Tres Torres

---

◗ *Rolling Catalan countryside, Alt Penedès*

Tarragona & the Costa Daurada

It would be a shame to visit Barcelona without seeing some of the sights of Catalonia with its beautiful landscapes and wide variety of attractions, which range from wine-tasting to roller-coaster rides. To the west, the Monestir de Montserrat is one of the most visited sights in Catalonia. South of Barcelona, the **Costa Daurada (Golden Coast)** is flanked by wide sandy beaches. Along with the popular wine-producing towns of Vilafranca del Penedès and Sant Sadurni d'Anoia, the two main destinations to visit here are Sitges, a delightful resort town that has a huge gay following, and the beautiful city of Tarragona, whose archaeological complex of ancient Roman treasures are a UNESCO World Heritage Site.

SIGHTS & ATTRACTIONS

Beaches
The Costa Daurada takes its name 'Golden Coast' from its broad sandy beaches and is within easy reach of Barcelona and Tarragona. Its resorts, including Salou, Altafulla, Torredembarra, Coma-Ruga and Vilanova i la Geltrú, have a traditional seaside atmosphere and are hugely popular with families.
ⓦ www.costadaurada.org

Montserrat
Montserrat is located 56 km (35 miles) north-west of Barcelona, at the summit of Catalonia's 1,200 m (4,000 ft) holy mountain (named after its strangely serrated rock formations: *mont*, mountain; *serrat*, sawed). Dramatically perched at the top of the mountain is one of Spain's most revered pilgrimage sites – the Monestir de Montserrat.

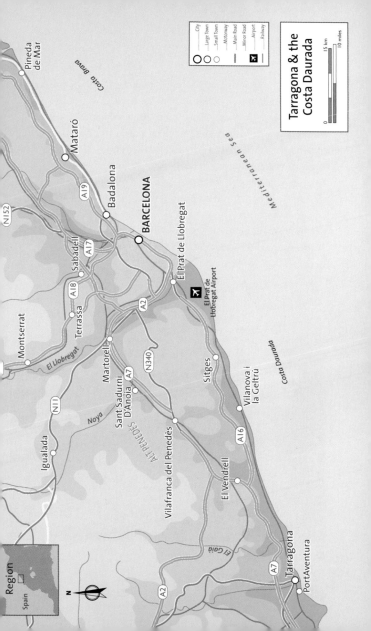

Costa Brava

Pineda
de Mar

Mataró

N152

Badalona

A19

BARCELONA

Sabadell

A7

A18

El Prat de Llobregat

Terrassa

Montserrat

A2

El Prat de
Llobregat Airport

El Llobregat

Mediterranean sea

Martorell

N340

Sant Sadurní
D'Anoia   A7

Sitges

Costa Daurada

NII

Noya

Igualada

ALT PENEDÈS

Vilanova i
la Geltrú

A16

Vilafranca del Penedès

El Vendrell

Region

Spain

N

El Gaià

A2

Tarragona

A7

PortAventura

Every year, thousands of worshippers take the thrilling cable-car ride up the mountain to venerate a small medieval statue of the Madonna and Child in the church, called *La Moreneta* (The Black Virgin), thought to have been made by St Luke and brought here by St Peter. The statue has been blackened by centuries of smoke from the millions of candles lit in her honour. The monastery also contains some important paintings by El Greco and Caravaggio and every day at 13.00 one of Europe's oldest boys' choirs, La Escolania, sings in the church.

☎ 938 777 701 ⏱ 08.00–10.30, 12.00–18.30 (church); 10.00–18.00 Mon–Fri, 09.30–18.30 Sat–Sun (museum)

🌐 www.abadiamontserrat.net

⬤ *The ancient vineyards of Alt Penedès*

Alt Penedès

Just half an hour's drive from Barcelona, the Alt Penedès is one of Spain's foremost wine-producing areas. Its two main towns, Sant Sadurní d'Anoia and Vilafranca del Penedès, have been producing wine since ancient times.

Vilafranca del Penedès is especially attractive with beautiful arcaded streets, medieval mansions and an atmospheric Gothic quarter. Here too is the **Museu del Vi** (Wine Museum), showing the history and techniques of wine-making in Catalonia. The three main wineries (Mas Tinell, Romagosa Torné and Miguel Torres) are all located on the outskirts (in the direction of Sant Marti Sarroca), and offer tours and wine-tastings (phone for details).

Nearby, Sant Sadurní d'Anoia is the centre of Catalonia's *cava* industry, with numerous producers dotted throughout the town. The largest, Codorníu, produces over 40 million bottles a year and its impressive *Modernista* plant is open to visitors for tours and tastings.

Codorníu ☎ 938 913 342 🌐 www.codorniu.es

Mas Tinell ☎ 938 170 586 🌐 www.mastinell.com

Miguel Torres ☎ 938 177 400 🌐 www.torres.es

Museu del Vi 📍 Plaça Jaume I 1–3, Vilafranca del Penedès ☎ 938 900 582

Romagosa Torné ☎ 938 991 353 🌐 www.romagosatorne.com

Sant Sadurni d'Anoia Tourist Office 📍 Carrer Hospital 26 ☎ 938 913 188 🌐 www.santsadurni.org

Vilafranca del Penedès Tourist Office 📍 Carrer Cort 14 ☎ 938 920 358 🌐 www.vilafranca.org

PortAventura

A short distance south of Barcelona near Tarragona, PortAventura, reputedly one of Europe's biggest and best theme parks, is

Catalunya's answer to Disneyland and is an entertaining day out for all the family, with its exotic shows and fairground rides in themed Mexican, Chinese, Polynesian, Wild West and Mediterranean settings. Don't miss the Dragon Khan, Europe's largest roller-coaster with a stomach-churning eight 360° loops.

ⓐ PortAventura, near Tarragon ① 977 779 090 ① 10.00–20.00 Mar–June, Sept–Oct; 10.00–24.00 July & Aug. Check website for other opening times ⓦ www.portaventura.es

---

THE LOCAL TIPPLE

The Alt Penedès region produces excellent red (*tinto* or *negra*), white (*blanc*) and rosé (*rosat*) wines as well as Catalan champagne, called *cava*. Look out also for *xampanyerías* (champagne bars), which serve house *cavas* by the glass. They are labelled according to quality and sweetness – *brut nature*, *brut*, *sec* and *semi-sec* (which despite its name is very sweet and the cheapest).

Sitges

Just 40 km (25 miles) south of Barcelona, the attractive beach resort of Sitges has long been a holiday playground of Barcelonans, celebrated for its beautiful Platja d'Or (Golden Beach) which stretches southwards for 5 km (3 miles) from the baroque church of Sant Bartomeu i Santa Tecla. The old town itself is full of bohemian charm, with its narrow streets of flower-bedecked whitewashed cottages, and attractive *Modernista* buildings. From the mid-19th century, Sitges attracted artists and writers, including *Modernista* painter Santiago Rusinyol, whose villa – Cau Ferrat – is now a museum. The palm-fringed promenade is lined with beach bars, cafés and fish

restaurants. However, Sitges is perhaps best known today for its vibrant nightlife. It is also a popular gay holiday destination.
Tourist Office ⓐ Carrer Sínia Morera 1 ⓒ 938 945 004
ⓦ www.sitgestur.com

CULTURE

Tarragona
Located on a rocky bluff just 97 km (60 miles) south-west of Barcelona, Tarragona boasts the largest ensemble of Roman remains in Spain – the extraordinary architectural legacy of Roman *Tarraco*, former capital of the Iberian peninsula. The Romans captured Tarragona in 218 BC and it became the home of Julius Caesar, and the base for the Roman conquest of Spain. It was also the main commercial centre on this stretch of coast until the 12th century, when Barcelona overshadowed it following the Christian reconquest of the nation.

🔻 *The Platja d'Or and church of Sant Bartomeu i Santa Tecla at Sitges*

The Roman remains in the city are remarkable. The **Amfiteatre Roma** is cut into the hillside overlooking the Mediterranean. This is where the Romans held their public spectacles, including gladiator fights, before an audience of 12,000 people. During the 12th century, the Romanesque church of Santa Maria del Miracle was built on the site. The **Museu d'Història** (Tarragona History Museum) traces the history of the city through an astonishing array of ancient treasures, while the equally fascinating **Museu Nacional Arqueològic** (Archeological Museum) includes a section of the old Roman wall together with busts of emperors, sarcophagi and some beautiful mosaics. Walk the **Passeig Arqueològic**, a promenade around the Roman walls for excellent views of the city and the hinterland of the Camp de Tarragona.

A short walk from the city centre, the **Museu i Necropolia Palaeocristians** (Palaeo-Christian Museum) contains the city's most treasured Roman remains in a former necropolis, with superb mosaics, glass, pottery and ivory.

With so many Roman treasures, it would be easy to overlook Tarragona's mighty Cathedral – a magnificent Romanesque-Gothic construction in the form of a cross, created at the highest point of the city as the centrepiece of the *ciutat antiga* (old city).

Amfiteatre Roma ❸ Parc del Miracle ❶ 977 242 220 ❷ 09.00–21.00 Easter week–Sept; 09.00–17.00 Oct–Easter

Catedral ❸ Plaça de la Seu ❶ 977 238 685 ❷ 10.00–13.00, 16.00–19.00 Mon–Sat, mid-Mar–May; 10.00–19.00 Mon–Sat, June–mid-Oct; 10.00–17.00 Mon–Sat, mid-Oct–mid-Nov; 10.00–14.00 Mon–Sat, mid-Nov–mid-Mar

Museu d'Història ❸ Plaça del Rei ❶ 977 236 209 ❷ 09.00–21.00 Tues–Sat, 09.00–15.00 Sun, June–Sept; 10.00–13.30, 15.30–18.30 Tues–Sat, 10.00–14.00 Sun, Oct–May

Museu Nacional Arqueològic @ Plaça del Rei 5 ☏ 977 236 209
Museu i Necropolia Palaeocristians @ Passeig de la Independència
☏ 977 211 175
Passeig Arqueològic @ El Portal del Roser ☏ 977 245 796
🕒 09.00–21.00 Tues–Sat, 09.00–15.00 Sun, May–Sept; 09.00–19.00
Tues–Sun, Oct–Mar
Tarragona Tourist Office @ Carrer Major 39 ☏ 977 250 795
🌐 www.tarragonaturisme.es

Villa Casals, Sant Salvador

The celebrated Barcelonan cellist, Pablo Casals (1876–1973), built a
summer residence near the beach in the delightful town of Sant
Salvador. Today it contains a museum in his honour, documenting
the life and work of this musical genius. A veritable child prodigy, he
started out on a home-made instrument constructed from a broom
handle, a large gourd and some gut strings, and by the age of four
he could play the violin, piano, flute and organ. His solo debut in
Paris in 1899 launched him on a touring career that made him

🔺 *Tarragona – the atmospheric old city*

famous worldwide. Eventually, in 1920 he started conducting and founded his own orchestra in Barcelona until 1939, when he was forced into exile. He never returned to his house here, but one year after his death it was inaugurated as a museum.

ⓐ Avinguda Palfuriana 59, Sant Salvador ⓣ 977 684 276
ⓛ 10.00–14.00, 16.00–18.00 Tues–Fri, 10.00–14.00, 16.00–19.00 Sat, 10.00–14.00 Sun, mid-Sept–mid-June; 10.00–14.00, 17.00–21.00 Tues–Sat, 10.00–14.00 Sun, mid-June–mid-Sept
ⓦ www.paucasals.org

RETAIL THERAPY

Shopping here doesn't match Barcelona for choice or style, but Tarragona has some reasonable shops and fashion boutiques, most notably along La Rambla Nova and in the Centro Comercial Parc Central on Avinguda Roma. Sitges has some quirky boutiques and fun gift shops, and be sure to stop at one of the many wineries in Vilafranca del Penedès or Sant Sadurní di Anoia, to stock up your wine cellar.

TAKING A BREAK

Coma-Ruga
Casa Victor £ A popular tapas bar, adjoining a smart seafood restaurant on the seafront. ⓐ Passeig Maritim 23 ⓣ 977 681 473

Vilafranca del Penedès
Sant Jordi – Ca La Katy £–££ This rural restaurant, with its hearty helpings of traditional dishes, is always a popular lunch stop.
ⓐ BP2121 Vilafranca – Sant Martí Sarroca ⓣ 938 991 153

AFTER DARK

Restaurants
Montserrat
Abat Cisneros ££ Traditional Catalan specialities in former 16th-century monastery stables. ⓐ Hotel Abat Cisneros, Plaça de Monestir ⓣ 938 777 701

Sitges
Mare Nostrum ££ Sophisticated fish restaurant on the seafront. Try the special Xato de Sitges (grilled fish with romesco sauce). ⓐ Passeig de la Ribera 60–2 ⓣ 938 943 393

Tarragona
Sol-Ric ££ Cosy restaurant serving traditional dishes and superb seafood, on the outskirts of town. ⓐ Via Augusta 227 ⓣ 977 232 032

Estacio Marítima £££ Top-notch fish restaurant in the atmospheric fishermen's district of Serralló. ⓐ Moll de Costa Tinglado 4 ⓣ 977 232 759

Vilafranca del Penedès
Cal Ton ££ Modern minimalist restaurant serving inspiring Catalan cuisine with a twist. ⓐ Carrer del Casal 8 ⓣ 938 903 741

Nightlife
There are plenty of outdoor cafés and bars in the beach resorts and Tarragona, some of which have live music. Sitges is renowned for its gay scene, with dozens of gay bars in Carrer Sant Bonaventura alone. Mediterráneo (ⓐ Carrer Sant Bonaventura 6) is the largest

gay disco. Other popular venues (for gay and straight clubbers) include Ricky's (Carrer Sant Pau 25) and Trailer (Carrer Angel Vidal 36), with its infamous foam parties.

ACCOMMODATION

Montserrat
Abat Cisneros £ A pleasant 3-star hotel with cheap, basic rooms in former monks' cells. ⓐ Plaça de Monestir ⓣ 938 350 201

Sitges
El Xalet £ This small tranquil hotel is housed in a beautiful *Modernista* villa with an outdoor pool and garden. ⓐ Carrer Illa de Cuba 33–5 ⓣ 938 110 070

Celimar £–££ A small hotel in a beautiful *Modernista* building facing the sea. ⓐ Passeig de Ribera 20 ⓣ 938 110 170 ⓦ www.hotelcelimar.com

Dolce Sitges £££ Stay with the beautiful people at this cutting-edge new 5-star hotel on the outskirts of town. ⓐ Avinguda Camí de Miralpeix 12 ⓣ 938 109 000 ⓦ www.sitges.dolce.com

Tarragona
Husa Imperial Tarraco ££ The best hotel in town, with superb views of the coast and the Roman amphitheatre. ⓐ Passeig Palmeres ⓣ 977 233 040 ⓦ www.husa.es

ⓞ *Telephone box in Barcelona*

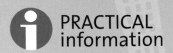

PRACTICAL
information

Directory

GETTING THERE

By air

Barcelona's El Prat de Llobregat Airport (**ⓘ** 932 983 838
Ⓦ www.aena.es Ⓔ bcninformacion@aena.es) is increasingly well
served by low-cost airlines from various UK and European
destinations. The airport has three terminals (A, B and C), all linked
by a walkway. Foreign airlines mostly use terminal A while Iberia, the
national airline, generally uses terminal B. Terminal C is used mainly
for domestic flights. There are easy connections to the city by bus,
train and taxi.

The flight time from London is approximately two hours. If you
are struggling to find a cheap ticket, it is also worth considering
flying with Ryanair, or a charter company such as First Choice
Airways, into Girona-Costa Brava airport, which is only 112 km
(70 miles) away – just one and a half hours by car or train to
Barcelona. Ryanair also flies into Reus, some 100 km (65 miles) south
of Barcelona. The best deals can be found by booking well in advance
through the websites of leading airlines and tour operators.

Visitors from the USA can fly directly with Iberia, or take a
connecting flight in Madrid or one of the other main European hubs.

British Airways **ⓘ** (UK) 0870 850 9850, (Spain) 902 111 333
Ⓦ www.britishairways.com

easyJet **ⓘ** (Barcelona) 933 792 720 **Ⓦ** www.easyjet.com

First Choice Airways **ⓘ** (UK) 0870 850 3999 **Ⓦ** www.firstchoice.co.uk

Iberia **ⓘ** (UK) 0870 609 0500, (Spain) 902 400 500 **Ⓦ** www.iberia.com

Ryanair **ⓘ** (Girona and Reus) 972 473 650 **Ⓦ** www.ryanair.com

Many people are aware that air travel emits CO_2 which contributes
to climate change. You may be interested in the possibility of

lessening the environmental impact of your flight through the charity Climate Care, which offsets your CO_2 by funding environmental projects around the world. Visit www.climatecare.org

By road

The usual route from the UK by car involves driving down through France and across the Pyrenees to Barcelona. It is advisable to plan your route in advance with a detailed map and to allow at least two days for the journey. Remember to drive on the right, wear your seatbelt at all times and stick to the speed limits: 120 kph (74 mph) on motorways, 100 kph (62 mph) on dual carriageways, 90 kph (56 mph) on other roads, except in urban areas where it is 50 kph (31 mph) unless otherwise stated.

The journey from London to Barcelona by coach takes around 26 hours. Contact Eurolines for further information.
Eurolines ⓣ (UK) 08705 143219, (Spain) 902 405 040
ⓦ www.eurolines.es

By rail

RENFE, the Spanish rail network, links Barcelona to Madrid and other major cities in Spain and abroad. Seat reservations are required on all intercity trains. It takes just 15 hours by train from London via the Channel Tunnel to Barcelona. Contact Rail Europe for further information.
Rail Europe ⓦ www.raileurope.com
RENFE ⓣ 902 240 202 ⓐ www.renfe.es

By sea

The Port de Barcelona is the second largest cruise centre in the Mediterranean after Athens. There are a total of five cruise ship terminals (two at Moll Adossat, two at Moll Barcelona and one at Moll Espanya), each with tourist information centres, bureaux de change, first-aid facilities, car hire, shops, bars and restaurants.

There are also regular ferries from the Balearic islands of Mallorca, Menorca and Ibiza, operated by Trasmediterránea, as well as a fast ferry service between Palma and Barcelona.

Autoritat Portuària de Barcelona Ⓦ www.apb.es

Trasmediterránea ☎ 902 454 645 Ⓦ www.trasmediterranea.es

TRAVEL INSURANCE

Whichever mode of transport you choose, make sure you have adequate personal travel insurance for the trip. The policy should give cover for medical expenses, loss, theft, repatriation, personal liability and cancellation expenses. If you are travelling in your own vehicle, you should also check that you are properly insured, and remember to take your driving licence and all relevant insurance documents with you.

ENTRY FORMALITIES

Citizens of EU countries, USA, Canada, Australia, New Zealand, South Africa and Ireland who hold valid passports do not need a visa to visit Spain for less than 90 days. Other visitors should check with their nearest Spanish consulate.

Visitors to Barcelona from within the EU are entitled to bring their personal effects and goods for personal consumption and not for resale, up to a total of 800 cigarettes and 10 litres of spirits. Duty-free limits for those entering from outside the EU are 200 cigarettes (50 cigars, 250 g tobacco), 1 litre of spirits or 2 litres of wine. No meat or dairy produce is permitted into the country from inside or outside the EU.

MONEY

Spain's currency is the euro, with notes issued in denominations of 5, 10, 20, 50 and 100 euros, and coins of 1 and 2 euros and also 1, 2, 5, 10, 20 and 50 cents. Credit cards are widely used in Barcelona (especially VISA, MasterCard, AMEX and Diners Club) and most UK banks' cash cards can be used to obtain cash in local currency from some ATMs, although the commission charged can be expensive.

HEALTH, SAFETY & CRIME

The water in Barcelona is safe to drink although most people prefer to drink bottled water – either still (*agua sin gas*) or carbonated (*agua con gas*). A change of diet could lead to stomach upsets, so carry a supply of anti-diarrhoea tablets just in case.

Thanks to a reciprocal healthcare agreement, nationals of EU countries and some other countries can get reduced-price, sometimes free, medical treatment in Spain on presentation of a valid European Health Insurance Card (EHIC), the replacement for the E111 which ceased to be valid on 31 December 2005. This card gives access to state-provided medical treatment only. Apply online for an EHIC at www.dh.gov.uk/travellers and allow at least 2–3 weeks until you receive the card. On top of this, private medical insurance is still advised and is essential for all other visitors. If you need to consult an English-speaking doctor, ask for help at your hotel reception or call the Centre Mèdic Assistencial de Catalunya (ⓐ Carrer Provença 281 ⓣ 932 153 793 ⓛ 08.00–20.00 Mon–Fri (See also page 156 for emergency medical aid.)

Violent crime is rare in Barcelona but the petty crime rate (pick-pocketing, purse-snatching, etc) is high, especially in the Barri Gòtic around Plaça Reial and in El Raval. Don't carry excess cash, and use the hotel safe for valuable goods; don't leave anything visible in a parked car; beware of pickpockets in crowded places (especially on La Rambla); and stick to well-lit populated areas by night. The Policía Municipal (in navy-blue uniforms) keep law and order in the city and are generally helpful. If you need a police station, ask for *la comisaría*. (See also page 156 for emergency police assistance.)

OPENING HOURS

Banks: Most banks open 08.30–14.00 Mon–Fri. Some main branches also open 08.30–12.30 on Saturdays.

Businesses: Business hours are generally 08.00/09.00–18.00/19.00 Mon–Fri, with a siesta around 13.30–15.30/16.00.

Museums: Museum hours vary. Museums close for the lunchtime siesta and some close early on Sunday.

Shops: Most shops open 09.00/10.00 until around 14.00, then again around 16.30–20.00/21.00. Some open on Saturday mornings, but very few open on Saturday afternoons or Sundays. Market times vary, but the city's food markets (including La Boqueria) are generally open every morning Mon–Sat.

TOILETS

It is difficult to find public toilets in the city, so you are best advised to rely on the facilities provided in museums, galleries, shops, bars and restaurants, which are usually free.

CHILDREN

Children receive a warm welcome in Barcelona, and they are welcomed rather than tolerated in cafés, restaurants and even bars. Many restaurants offer special children's menus or portions. Nappies, baby food and formula milk can be bought from supermarkets but, if you have a preferred brand take a supply with you. If you need to hire a car seat for a child, double-check availability when making the booking and also check the seat carefully before fitting. Ask your hotel reception about babysitters and local crèches. Some hotels offer a room-listening service for the evenings.

There are great parks and playgrounds for children to enjoy throughout the city, and lovely sandy beaches. Many of the museums and attractions also appeal to children and even some of the city's transportation modes are entertaining, especially the cable cars and funiculars. The following activities are guaranteed to keep the kids entertained:

- **L'Aquàrium** (see page 72) Special hands-on exhibits and a fascinating underwater tunnel.

- **Beaches** (see page 72) Beautiful sandy beaches with playgrounds, shops, showers and lifeguards. At Nova Mar Bella, there are small boats for hire in summer.

- **Camp Nou** (see page 120) One of the world's biggest football stadiums and home to FC Barça.

- **Cosmocaixa** (see page 124) Fun and games at the spectacular new science museum and planetarium, appealing to all ages.

- **La Font Màgica** (see page 109) A spectacular sound-and-light extravaganza.

- **PortAventura** (see page 133) One of Europe's largest theme parks, just south of Tarragona.

- **Las Golondrinas** (see page 74) Boat trips around the harbour and to the Olympic port.

- **IMAX** (see page 86) Larger than life movies.

- **MACBA** (see page 112) Older children find the modern art installations amusing.

- **Museu d'Història de Catalunya** (see page 79) This state-of-the-art educational museum is great fun for older children, with loads of interactive sections.

- **Museu Marítim** (see page 114) It's fun to climb aboard the boats and to experience life at sea.

- **Parc d'Atraccions, Tibidabo** (see page 123) Old-fashioned fairground on top of Mont Tibidabo.

- **Parc de la Ciutadella** (see page 76) A boating lake and a life-size elephant statue.

- **Parc Zoològic** (see page 77) The city zoo appeals to children young and old.

- **Poble Espanyol** (see page 109) Hunt for souvenirs in the shops of this 'Spanish Village'.

- **La Rambla** (see page 58) Small children find the street entertainments fascinating here.

COMMUNICATIONS
Phones

Public phones are easy to use. Most take coins, phone cards and credit cards and they have instructions for use in English: basically lift the receiver, insert payment and dial the number. Phone cards can be purchased from post offices, tobacconists and many other shops. Spain has an excellent mobile phone network. If you plan to use your mobile abroad, check with your service provider that you will be able to access the relevant networks.

The Spanish Yellow Pages (*Páginas Amarillas*, ⓦ www.paginasamarillas.es), is a useful source for telephone numbers.

International enquiries ☎ 11825
National enquiries ☎ 11818
Operator ☎ 1002

TELEPHONING SPAIN
To phone Spain from abroad, dial the international access code (00) followed by the country code 34. All telephone numbers in Barcelona begin with 93 followed by a seven-digit number.

TELEPHONING ABROAD
To phone home from Barcelona, dial the international access code (00) followed by the relevant country code: UK 44, USA and Canada 1, Australia 61, New Zealand 64, Republic of Ireland 353, South Africa 72, then the local code (minus the initial 0) and finally the number you want.

⬤ *The Plaça d'Espanya is one of the city's major traffic intersections*

Post

The Spanish postal service is moderately efficient and its bright yellow offices (*Correos*) and postboxes are easy to spot. The central post office is at Via Laietana 1, and is open 08.30–21.00 Mon–Sat, 08.00–14.00 Sun. Stamps can be purchased at post offices and tobaconnists. It costs €0.53 to send a postcard to Europe and €0.78 to the rest of the world.

Internet cafés

Many hotels and hostels now offer internet access and there are cybercafés dotted all over the city including:

Bar Daguiri A bar by the beach with free internet access. Bring along your laptop and they will wire you up. ⓐ Carrer Grau i Torras 59
ⓘ 932 215 109 Ⓜ Metro: Barceloneta

Bornet A popular internet café in front of the Picasso Museum. ⓐ Barra de Ferro 3 📞 933 194 698

Electric Lounge An internet café-lounge by the cathedral, with free coffee. 📞 Carrer Misser Ferrer 1 📞 933 041 616
🌐 www.electric-barcelona.com

ELECTRICITY

Electricity is supplied at 220–5 volts. Spanish plugs are of the two-pin round plug variety, so an adapter will be required for British and non-Continental appliances. US and other visitors with 110-volt appliances will need to use a voltage transformer too.

TRAVELLERS WITH DISABILITIES

Most of the city's modern attractions (such as MACBA and Cosmocaixa), along with many buses and the newest metro line 2 (purple), have good access for those with disabilities. However, in the narrow streets and ancient buildings of the historic centre and in some of the *Modernista* houses, access is poor. All new buildings are now, by law, disabled-friendly. For taxis adapted to persons with reduced mobility, 📞 934 208 088. The tourist offices can provide further useful addresses.

For further information contact:

Disabled Persons Transport Advisory Committee (UK)
🌐 www.dptac.gov.uk/door-to-door

Society for Accessible Travel & Hospitality (STH) Advice for US-based travellers with disabilities. 📞 212 447 7284
🌐 www.sath.org

Trip Scope Advice for UK-based travellers with disabilities. 📞 08457 585641 🌐 www.tripscope.org.uk

FURTHER INFORMATION

Barcelona's Tourist Information Offices (*Turisme de Barcelona*) are useful for maps, accommodation, attractions and event information and any other queries you have about the city. There are several branches:

Airport ● Terminals A & B ● 09.00–21.00, closed 25 Dec and 1 Jan

Plaça de Catalunya ● Plaça de Catalunya 17–S (main office) ● 09.00–21.00, closed 1 Jan and 25 Dec

Plaça Sant Jaume ● Carrer Ciutat 2 ● 09.00–20.00 Mon–Fri, 10.00–20.00 Sat, 10.00–14.00 Sun and public holidays

Sants Railway Station ● Plaça Països Catalans ● 08.00–20.00 (summer); 08.00–20.00 Mon–Fri, 08.00–14.00 Sat & Sun and public holidays (winter), closed 25–6 Dec, 1 Jan

There are also a number of information booths at strategic points around the city:

Barceloneta ● Plaça Joan de Borbó ● 10.00–20.00 July–Sept; weekends only in winter

Columbus Monument ● Plaça Portal de la Pau ● 09.00–21.00

Estació del Nord ● Carrer Alí Bei 80 ● 09.30–14.30 Mon–Sat

Plaça Espanya ● Avinguda Maria Cristina/Plaça Espanya ● 10.00–20.00 July–Sept; 10.00–16.00 Oct–June

Sagrada Família ● Carrer Sardenya (in front of the Passion façade) ● 10.00–20.00 July–Sept; 10.00–16.00 Oct–June

The tourist office also has a multilingual call centre for general tourist information ● 807 117 222 (from Spain); 932 853 834 (from abroad). Their official website, together with the Spanish National Tourist Office, provides further details (in English, French, Spanish and Catalan) about the city and the region, its history, events and facilities.

Spanish National Tourist Office Ⓦ www.tourspain.es
Turisme de Barcelona Ⓦ www.barcelonaturisme.com

For further information on the city's acclaimed *Modernista* architecture and the *Ruta del Modernisme* (a self-guided walking route past many of the city Modernist highlights), contact the Centre del Modernisme.
ⓐ Casa Amatller, Passeig de Gràcia 41 ⓣ 934 880 139

BACKGROUND READING

An Olympic Death, Manuel Vázquez Montalbán – crime novel, written just before the 1992 Olympics, with a Barcelona native as the central detective character.

Barcelona Design Guide, Juliet Pomés Leiz & Ricardo Feriche – a comprehensive guide to Barcelona's 'designer' culture.

Barcelona: The Great Enchantress, Robert Hughes – a 21st-century portrait of the city.

Barcelonas, Manuel Vázquez Montalbán – reflections on the city by one of its most prominent modern authors.

The Best of Worlds, Quim Monzo – black humour with Barcelona as its backdrop, by Catalonia's best-selling author.

Homage to Barcelona, Colm Tóibín – a fascinating account of the city, its art and architecture.

Homage to Catalonia, George Orwell – first-hand observations of life in the region during the Spanish Civil War.

The Shadow of the Wind, Carlos Ruiz Zafón – this mystery story set in 1950s Barcelona was a runaway bestseller.

The Time of the Doves, Merce Rodoreda – novel set in the city during the Civil War, by one of Catalonia's most celebrated women writers.

Useful phrases: Catalan & Spanish

Barcelona is a bilingual city with two official languages, Catalan and (Castilian) Spanish. Catalan is not a dialect but a distinct language with a long and proud history. It is spoken by over six million people and understood by ten million (in Catalonia, Valencia, the Balearic islands, Roussillon in southern France, Andorra, and Alghero in Sardinia). Most Barcelonans are bilingual and switch back and forth between Catalan and Spanish depending on who they are talking to.

Most hotel, museum and tourist office staff will speak some English but any attempt to speak Spanish, rather than English, will go down well. However, if you can manage a few words of Catalan, you'll really win people over.

English	Catalan	Spanish
BASICS		
Yes	Si	Si
No	No	No
Please	Si us plau	Por favor
Sorry	Perdoni	Perdone
Thank you	Gràcies	Gracias
Bon appetit	Bon profit	Buen provecho
Hello	Hola	Hola
How are you?	Com estàs?	¿Cómo estás?
Goodbye	Adéu	Adiós
Morning	Matí	Mañana
Good morning	Bon dia	Buenos días
Afternoon/evening	Tarda	Atarde
Good afternoon/evening	Bona tarda	Buenas tardes
Night	Nit	Noche
Good night	Bona nit	Buenas noches
I don't speak Catalan/Spanish	No parla català/espanyol	No hablo catalán/español

English	Catalan	Spanish
Do you speak English?	Parla anglès?	¿Habla inglés?
I don't understand	No ho entenc	No entiendo
Where is ...?	On està ...?	¿Donde está ...?
How much is ...?	Quant val ...?	¿Cuánto cuesta ...?
Breakfast	Esmorzar	Desayuno
Lunch	Dinar	Almuerzo
Dinner	Sopar	Cena
Open	Obert	Abierto
Closed	Tancat	Cerrado

DAYS OF THE WEEK

Monday	Dilluns	Lunes
Tuesday	Dimarts	Martes
Wednesday	Dimecres	Miércoles
Thursday	Dijous	Jueves
Friday	Divendres	Viernes
Saturday	Dissabte	Sábado
Sunday	Diumenge	Domingo

NUMBERS

One	U (un, una)	Uno
Two	Dos	Dos
Three	Tres	Tres
Four	Quatre	Cuatro
Five	Cinc	Cinco
Six	Sis	Seis
Seven	Set	Siete
Eight	Vuit	Ocho
Nine	Nou	Nueve
Ten	Deu	Diez
Eleven	Onze	Once
Twelve	Dotze	Doce
Twenty	Vint	Veinte
Fifty	Cinquanta	Cincuenta
One hundred	Cent	Cien

See also the Spanish phrases for specific situations in other parts of this book.

Emergencies

EMERGENCY NUMBERS
Ambulance ❶ 061
Emergency (Catalonia) ❶ 112
Fire ❶ 080
Guardia Urbana (City police) ❶ 092
Mossos d'Esquadra (Emergencies and traffic accidents) ❶ 088
Policía Nacional (National police) ❶ 091

MEDICAL SERVICES
Should you become seriously ill, lists of local doctors (*medicos*), dentists (*dentistas*) and hospitals can be found in telephone directories or by contacting your consulate, who will have lists of English-speaking practitioners. Alternatively, ask your hotel reception to help or, in a real emergency, dial 061 for an ambulance. If you have a valid European Health Insurance Card (EHIC, see page 145), you should ensure that the doctor is part of the Spanish healthcare system as the card covers only state-provided medical treatment.

Pharmacies (*farmàcias*) are widespread, and their highly trained staff can provide medical advice and over-the-counter drugs. In an emergency, go straight to the city centre casualty department, Centre d'Urgències Perecamps ❷ Avinguda de les Drassanes 13–15 ❶ 934 410 600 Ⓜ Metro: Drassanes

THE POLICE
There are several police stations (open 24 hours) throughout the city including:

Barceloneta: Passeig Joan de Borbó 32 ☏ 932 240 600
Eixample: Carrer de Guadalajara 3 ☏ 932 903 021
El Raval: Carrer Nou de la Rambla 78–80 ☏ 932 902 844

There is also a multilingual police service at the Guardia Urbana station on La Rambla near Plaça Reial.
Guardia Urbana de Ciutat Vella ⓐ La Rambla 43 ☏ 932 562 430

CONSULATES & EMBASSIES

Australian ⓐ Plaça Gala Placidia 1, Barcelona ☏ 934 309 013
British ⓐ Avinguda Diagonal 477, Barcelona ☏ 933 666 200
Canadian ⓐ Carrer Elisenda de Pinós 10, Barcelona ☏ 932 042 700
Irish ⓐ Gran Via Carlos III, 94, Barcelona ☏ 934 915 021
New Zealand ⓐ Travesera de Gràcia 64, Barcelona ☏ 932 090 399
South African ⓐ Carrer Claudio Coello 91, Madrid ☏ 91 436 3780
United States ⓐ Passeig Reina Elisenda Montcada 23, Barcelona ☏ 932 802 227

DRIVING

Breakdown services and motoring information can be obtained from the Real Automobile Club de Catalunya (RACC), Avenida Diagonal 687 ☏ 934 955 050 for 24-hour information and emergency breakdown service ⓦ www.racc.es

> **EMERGENCY PHRASES IN SPANISH**
> **(See also pages 154–5)**
>
> **Help!** ¡Socorro! *¡Sawkoro!*
> **Fire!** ¡Fuego! *¡Fwegoh!*
> **Stop!** ¡Stop! *¡Stop!*

The publishers would like to thank the following individuals and organisations for supplying the copyright photographs for this book.

Teresa Fisher: all photographs except page 124

Pictures Colour Library: page 124

Copy editor: Susan Hamilton
Proofreader: Lynn Bresler

Send your thoughts to
books@thomascook.com

- Found a great bar, club, shop or must-see sight that we don't feature?

- Like to tip us off about any information that needs updating?

- Want to tell us what you love about this handy little guidebook and more importantly how we can make it even handier?

Then here's your chance to tell all! Send us ideas, discoveries and recommendations today and then look out for your valuable input in the next edition of this title. As an extra 'thank you' from Thomas Cook Publishing, you'll be automatically entered into our exciting monthly prize draw.

Send an email to the above address (stating the book's title) or write to: CitySpots Project Editor, Thomas Cook Publishing, PO Box 227, The Thomas Cook Business Park, Unit 18, Coningsby Road, Peterborough PE3 8SB, UK.